What Price Coexistence?

By the same author:

AIR POWER AND ARMIES

STRATEGY FOR THE WEST

THE CENTRAL BLUE

THE GREAT DETERRENT

What
Price
Coexistence?

A Policy for the Western Alliance

Marshal of the Royal Air Force
SIR JOHN SLESSOR

FREDERICK A. PRAEGER, *Publisher*
New York

BOOKS THAT MATTER

First published in the United States of America in 1961 by
Frederick A. Praeger, Inc., Publisher
64 University Place, New York 3, N.Y.

© 1961 by Frederick A. Praeger, Inc.

Library of Congress Catalog Card Number: 61-13864

Manufactured in the United States of America

Contents

1 The Object 3

2 Know Your Enemy 14

3 Some Basic Principles 29

4 Disarmament—Illusion and Reality 44

5 The Home Front 57

6 First Steps in Europe 71

7 A New Plan for NATO 85

8 First Steps Toward Arms Control
and Political Adjustment in Europe 99

9 Global Strategy 112

10 Colonialism—The American Obsession 125

11 Western Strategy in the Middle East,
Far East, and Africa 133

Postscript on Berlin 148

What Price Coexistence?

Editor's Note: The major portion of this book was written by Sir John Slessor in January and February, 1961. Because of the highly topical nature of his theme, he has tried to take into account important developments since that time. His comments on these later events— written in mid-June, 1961, when the book was in proofs —appear as footnotes to the text. He has also added a Postscript on the Berlin situation as of June 15, 1961.

Chapter 1

The Object

De quoi s'agit il?

(MARSHAL FOCH)

THE EDUCATION of officers in the British fighting services—
and, no doubt, in those of other nations—includes instruction
in the art of writing an appraisal* of the various factors affecting a given military situation, leading up to the choice of a
plan of action.

I shall not attempt, in the chief space of this book, to provide anything like a comprehensive appreciation of the military situation in the world today. All I am setting out to do
is to state a personal view on some of the crucial political
and strategic issues facing us at this rather important stage
in the vast secular revolution of our age. But it does seem
desirable to begin—as students at staff colleges are taught to
do—by defining the object:† What is it we are trying to do,

---

* The accepted British term is "appreciation."

† Throughout this book, the words "object" and "objective" are used
in the sense defined in the *Concise Oxford Dictionary:* "object" being a
definition of policy or intention, "the thing aimed at, end, purpose";
"objective" having the more limited meaning of "a point to which the
advance of troops is directed." The word "troops" in the latter definition
is interpreted here more broadly as strategy or method, whether political
or military. Thus in Operation Overlord, the object could be defined as to
free Europe from Nazi domination, and the first objective as the seizure
of the Normandy beachheads.

what is the aim we want to achieve—in short, what is it all about, *de quoi s'agit il* (in the words of old Marshal Foch)?

It is obviously only common sense to begin in that way. But in a rather long experience with appraisals at all levels, I have found it not uncommon for the first, the object, paragraph to be either omitted altogether or so ill-defined that the subsequent consideration of the courses open to achieve it—and hence the plan of action—has been imprecise or inconclusive.

One is chary of using terms like "turning point in history." How often has one not heard it said in the last twenty years that the next six months (or the next twenty-four hours, or the next year) will be the critical period? Actually, in this day and age, every period is a critical one; that is no occasion either for alarm or for impetuous action. But as these words are being written, in the early months of 1961, things are happening that present rather special opportunities and good reasons for resolute initiatives. We have seen the beginning of a new era in United States leadership; we have heard the open declaration by the Communists at their November, 1960, conference in Moscow that the Cold War is to be intensified under the code name "peaceful coexistence"; the Atlantic Council has instructed the permanent staffs to undertake a reappraisal of NATO strategy in Europe and of the weapons required to make it effective; and the indications are that new moves will soon be made to cut a path through the jungle of disagreement in the direction of some practical measures of disarmament.

This, therefore, seems a suitable moment to take a fresh look at strategy for the West, to note where it has led us in the past decade, and to look for some signposts pointing out the road that lies before us in the next decade.

It is no use setting out on a journey unless we know our destination. We may know that it will take a long time to get there; but we must also know the direction in which we

want to travel, be aware of the obstacles we have to surmount, and decide on at least the first staging post on the
long road, whence we will be able to survey afresh the ter-
rain between us and our goal. And in making this survey, it
is just as well not to try to look too far ahead. We must be
clear—and in agreement with our companions on the journey
—about what point we want to reach. But if we try at the
outset to map out the whole route in detail, the obstacles
are liable to appear so formidable as to deter us from setting
out at all; and we tend to forget that the country ahead may
look very different from the top of the first pass, once we
have reached it.

Before discarding this simile of the journey, I should make
it clear that when I use the word "we," I refer to the ex-
pedition as a whole, not merely to any individual member—
not just Britain or the United States, France or Germany or
Italy, but the free nations of the West, particularly those
who are joined together in alliance. I do not mean to underrate the importance of other regional treaties when I add
that the vital core of the matter is NATO. Europe is very
far from being the only theater of the Cold War; but it is
the inner bastion, the keep of freedom—and if Europe goes,
everything goes.

Let us therefore first take a look at our object. This
book is concerned primarily with military policy; but it is
an ancient truism that strategy cannot be divorced from
policy. The old conception of war as a continuation of
policy tends to be misleading. War was not so much a continuation of policy as one method of putting it into effect.
It seems to me more important than ever in these days to be
clear about this. It is true that there have been nations in the
past (of whom, incidentally, Russia is not one) by whom
war was elevated almost to the status of a religion and regarded as something desirable in itself; prominent among

them, of course, was the old Germany, which did, indeed, perish by the sword. If the definition of policy as "a course of action adopted by a government"* is accepted in its narrowest sense, then I suppose war itself could be described as policy. But inherent in the adoption of any course of action by any government is the idea of an end, a purpose to be achieved; without that, no course of action makes any sense. The purpose of policy has been pursued in peacetime by diplomacy, by political and economic action, by treaties and trade agreements, by propaganda and subversion, even by the veiled threat of force; and it is generally true to say that only at the failure of those methods have governments resorted to war to attain their ends. This should be qualified by admitting that it has not always been true of petty wars between strong powers and weaker ones, wars which could not involve any very serious consequences for the aggressor; it was not true, for instance, of the U.S. Government in the Spanish-American War, or of the British Government of India in the Afghan War of 1839. But, while no less inexcusable, such wars were understandable in the ethical context of a bygone age. The general truth remains that where two powerful nations or combinations were concerned, a government did not abandon unwarlike pressure for open war —for invasion, bombing, and blockade—if it could achieve its political purpose without it. Not Bismarck, not Kaiser Wilhelm, not even Hitler would have resorted to the terrible arbitrament of war if they had believed that they could get what they wanted by other means short of it. What they wanted, the political purpose that has always actuated policy leading to war, was to create a situation in the world, or in a part of the world, that they thought would be more favorable to themselves. And it can be said that the willingness of a government to enforce its policy by war was always

---

* *Concise Oxford Dictionary.*

in direct ratio to the extent that it believed the outcome would be favorable to itself.

It may seem pedantic to insist on this, but it is a point of cardinal importance in the world of the 1960's. In the past, no responsible government voluntarily embarked upon war as an instrument of policy unless it was (rightly or wrongly) reasonably certain of being able to win it. And winning a war meant, for either side, not merely forcing the enemy to lay down his arms and accept terms, but *being successful in creating conditions more favorable to oneself than if there had not been a war*. In the old days, that ambition was realizable; it was permissible and, on the whole, not very dangerous to take the view that the required conditions could be created at the expense of other people, and at an acceptable cost to oneself. Today, in a world that has been shrunk by modern means of communication to the dimensions of a Hellenic city-state, and in which the existence of the hydrogen bomb holds out the possibility of almost universal extermination, that is no longer possible. There is not the remotest possibility today of anyone "winning a war" in that definition of the term.

I must digress here to emphasize that it was a definition applicable equally to the aggressor and to his victim—the assumption in the latter case being that the only alternative to taking up the challenge was the acceptance of terms regarded as intolerable. It is true that the conditions of life —or of whatever life should survive—at the end of a nuclear war could hardly be described as tolerable. And for that reason, there are people in the democratic countries (as there probably are in the Communist bloc, though they are not permitted to express themselves freely) who proclaim their view that anything, even abject surrender to nuclear blackmail and occupation by a Communist enemy, would be preferable to nuclear war. These people, or some of them, are no doubt sincere, and their view should at least be understood even if not respected. But I do not share it—nor do I believe it to be shared by more than an insignificant fraction of their fellow citizens. And I will not attempt to argue the case. It seems to me to be a matter for a man's individual conscience, something rooted in habits of thought that I am sure would not be altered by anything I could say in this book.

It is in the belief that there is no prospect in any future war of victory as defined above that I have, since 1953, repeatedly expressed the view that no one will again resort to total war as an instrument of policy as long as the nuclear deterrent exists on both sides. And with the same proviso, I believe it to be in the highest degree improbable that either protagonist in the Cold War will allow its conduct of international affairs to assume a form or be carried to a point where the possibility of total war becomes a real danger. But one must accept as not inconceivable—for reasons that I will enlarge on later—the risk of total war arising through escalation, by accident or miscalculation, or through unreasoning fear on one side or the other. Moreover, we cannot accept as an aim of policy the indefinite continuation of a state of affairs in which the enormous potentialities of modern science for the advancement of human happiness and progress are protected only by a balance of terror and matched only by their equal potentialities for human destruction. In simple terms, the world we live in today just does not make sense, and we must do something to change it.

From this, it surely follows that our ultimate objective must include the removal of the causes of war and the establishment of permanent peace among nations. That, of course, is a crashing platitude. But let me enlarge on it. It cannot mean peace at any price, as I have already hinted. It does not mean merely disarmament—let alone unilateral disarmament in the West, which would be stark lunacy. It does not mean what seems to be some people's ideal—purely relief from the possibility of nuclear extermination; real abolition of nuclear weapons would in itself simply mean that war could once again appear potentially profitable to an aggressor. Actually, even if nuclear armaments were discarded and stockpiles destroyed—which I believe to be totally impracticable without lasting political settlement of the tensions that divide the world—can anyone seriously believe that in the second half of the twentieth century another long war could be waged without calling them back into the armories of the combatants? Having fought through two "conventional" world wars in the last fifty years, I can see few attractions in the possibility of having to face a third; and if it did break out, it seems to me fantastic to suppose that it could continue for more than a limited period in what has been described as a "noncatastrophic" manner.

What then? Visionaries may dream of the lion and the lamb lying down together. There is nothing wrong with idealism; it is a desirable quality as long as the idealist does not allow his eyes to become starry and keeps his feet firmly on the ground. But politics is the art of the possible, and surely the most we can hope for in the foreseeable future is a tolerable form of peaceful coexistence, a genuine coexistence, and not the Communist kind, which implies the bloodless victory of Communism (bloodless, that is, for the Communists)—a coexistence in which different nations and political systems agree to make the best of it, at least tolerate each other's differences, and, in their own self-interest, cooperate in exploiting the benefits of technical and scientific progress.

Not a bad definition of such a state of coexistence would be the *Panch Shila*, the famous five principles to which Nehru and Chou En-lai are theoretically so attached: equality, sovereignty, noninterference in internal affairs, nonaggression, and the right of all people to choose their own way of life. A new Atlantic Charter might do worse than begin with an amalgam of that and the Four Freedoms.

But only the most cursory glance through the December, 1960, manifesto of the eighty-one Communist parties is needed to remind one that this would be a very long-range program indeed. In any case, it is incomplete as an object; and the four other principles have no chance of being respected as long as sovereignty is interpreted as a license for any individual nation to maintain armed forces capable of enforcing its will upon others. We are dealing with human beings, and, the human animal being what he is, there will never be lasting peace until it becomes physically impossible to resolve differences between nations by force. That means that our object must include disarmament, and disarmament can ultimately be ensured and enforced only by some form of world government with limited responsibilities, high among which must be included the preservation of international order by some form of international police.

There, then, is our ultimate political object. It is, as I have said, a very long-term aim. It is none the worse for that as long as we recognize it as such and, on the one hand, are not too ambitious to approach it by a strategy of limited objectives or, on the other, too complacent or disunited to take vigorous initiatives toward attaining them. It is, however, too general and imprecise, too remote to serve as an immediate political and strategic program for the near future. It is a destination, not the next staging post on the road. These broad generalizations, however acceptable in themselves, are not a substitute for a practical, progressive, and dynamic plan of action. They are the equivalent of the Allied aim in 1944 to free Europe from Nazi domination. What should be the modern equivalent of the Normandy beachheads?

The purpose of this book can be summarized thus: to examine some of the limited objectives that might determine our strategy in the next decade.

One last word about our object that I hope may forestall a criticism. Too often, we are told that it is useless to adopt this or that policy because the Russians will never agree to it. Do not let us be diverted from any policy we favor by considerations of that sort. It is not always easy to be sure, until we try, what the Russians will or will not agree to. In any event, the present leaders in the Kremlin (and, assuredly, they cannot last forever) will never agree to anything reasonable (as other people understand the word) unless they are compelled by pressure of events or can be convinced that agreement is in their interest as much as in that of others. In pursuing their policy, they never worry about whether the free world will agree. They have a perfectly consistent, clear, and above all long-range policy from which they never depart. They play their hand differently at different times as they think it suits them. They are experts at playing on the nerves of their opponents by fabricating crises. At one moment they will be grossly provocative, at the next they will coo like any dove—the Pavlovian technique of conflicting signals to bemuse their opponents. They are prepared to bide their time in their crazy conviction that the victory of Communism is inevitable. Their tactics change, but never their strategy; and the December manifesto should not have been needed to remind us that their aim is the destruction of so-called "capitalism," with a resulting Communist world dominated by Moscow. They pursue that aim consistently and relentlessly, with no holds barred, quite regardless of such minor considerations as truth or what other people might like or not like.

That may change as time goes on, and we should always be on the lookout for and ready to respond to any genuine —as opposed to merely tactical—modifications in Soviet policy. Meanwhile, the indispensable essential for us is that we should match the Kremlin in the clear, consistent, and forward-looking character of our policy, and pursue it just as relentlessly. We should not and need not copy all the tactics of Communism, but we have something to learn from them in the conduct of our strategy. Above all, we must regain and retain the initiative, which we may as well admit to having lost in the decade of the 1950's—not always dancing to their tune, not wondering fearfully what they are going to do next and how to counter it, but keeping them guessing about what we are going to do next and imposing upon them the necessity of defending *their* goal line. As Prime Minister Macmillan said in the House of Commons after the summit fiasco of May, 1960, "We have to take note of what is said, objectively and dispassionately, not allowing ourselves to get back into the old days that some remember only too well, of waiting week by week for pronouncements by foreign statesmen and then attuning our policies to their changing emphasis." While refraining ourselves from the dangerous folly of "brinkmanship," we should never allow exhibitions of it on the part of the Kremlin to deflect us from our purpose.

We must pursue our long-term policy with steadfast consistency, not allowing ourselves to be inhibited from doing what we believe to be right in our own interest and in that of other non-Communist nations by groundless fears of provoking the Russians into war. But the first essential is to have a policy. "If an ambitious political aim does not govern NATO's second decade, its purpose will be infirm, the tension between its various members will grow, and its strategic and military planning will be a hand-to-mouth affair."*

Let me end this chapter by repeating the adaptation of

---

* Alastair Buchan, *NATO in the 1960's* (London: The Institute for Strategic Studies; New York: Frederick A. Praeger, 1960).

Danton's words quoted by M. Spaak in a recent address to NATO parliamentarians: *"De l'audace, encore de l'audace, toujours de l'audace, et l'ouest sera sauvé"* ("Daring, more daring, always daring, and the West will be saved").

Chapter 2

Know Your Enemy

WHEN THE STAFF OFFICER writes an appraisal, his definition of the object is followed by an examination of the factors affecting its attainment, including the nature and probable action of the enemy. I have neither the time nor the qualifications to attempt anything like a comprehensive examination of the multitudinous factors which must be taken into account in formulating a plan to defeat militant Communism and achieve our ultimate purpose. But in this chapter, I will try to elaborate on some of the points raised in the previous one, and particularly to define in rather more detail what I believe to be the real nature of the menace with which we are faced.

It has been a characteristic of modern dictatorships to publish their programs, so that he who runs may read. Too often, the trouble is that we in the free countries don't read them. If we had studied more carefully in the past quarter of a century the speeches and writings of Hitler, Stalin, and Mao, we would have had fewer unpleasant surprises than we have had. The latest example of this sort of warning is the almost unbearably turgid manifesto issued from Moscow in December, 1960, after the meeting of the eighty-one Communist parties. It is an amazingly frank declaration of cold war. Not even thinly veiled by the usual Communist double talk, it is an open expression of implacable hostility to the Western world and all we stand for—a clear notification, if ever there was one, of their intention to intensify the struggle for the destruction of "capitalism" (meaning every political system other than Communism) by "peaceful competition" (which clearly means by every known method short of a hot war). If anyone doubts that our opponents' strategic object remains a Communist world dominated by Moscow— "the universally recognized vanguard of the world Communist movement"—then let him read this document.

I have heard it suggested that its aggressively belligerent tone was in deference to the more militant wing of Communism represented by Peking. It is well known that the Chinese by no means yet rule out total war as part of the program, but they have conceded that point in the wording of the manifesto, no doubt as a bow to the "invincible solidarity" of world Communism. Khrushchev, however, went out of his way after the conference—incidentally, at just about the same time as he was assuring President Kennedy of his wish to improve relations between the U.S. and the U.S.S.R.—to declare in an important speech that "peaceful coexistence . . . is a form of intense political, economic, and ideological struggle between the proletariat and the aggressive forces of imperialism" (i.e., everyone other than Communists). Anyone who still imagines, even after his performance in Paris and New York in 1960, that Mr. K. is really a jolly little man, a sort of Russian Mr. Pickwick, still full of the bounding energy of his soccer-playing youth, a mine of wise and earthy old Russian proverbs, had better think it over more carefully. True, the devil you know is better than the devil you don't know, and we might have something worse at the head of the Russian police state. But we should not be misled by the naïve gullibility of eminent globetrotters like Field Marshal Montgomery into accepting the image of these dictators that it obviously suits them to impose upon us.

Communist China certainly looms as a menace of increasing proportions (about which I will have something to say later in this book). But if the Communists universally recognize Moscow as the spearhead, let us so recognize it as well. The enemy who is determined to destroy us is not the Russian people, but the group of dedicated revolutionaries in the Kremlin; and the sooner we face realities and call that spade a spade, the better we will be able to counter and defeat their murderous designs. I use the word "murderous" advisedly. The logical and inevitable outcome of successful peaceful coexistence, as defined by Khrushchev, is not only the destruction of our institutions and way of life, but also enslavement, torture, and death for hundreds of thousands of men and women. It does not mean merely peaceful competition among the various peoples in trade, scientific, and cultural spheres, on the boards of the Bolshoi Theater or over the fences at Aintree; nobody minds that—indeed, we would welcome it. But what it really means is class struggle, bloody revolution, tanks in the streets, and the "liquidation" of political opponents, as in the cases of Nagy and Maleter —in short, just what we have witnessed, to our sorrow and shame, in a dozen formerly free countries of Europe in our generation.

That is the end to which militant Communism is already hard at work by psychological attack on the minds of men in other still free countries, including our own. Anyone with any modicum of intelligence who is not willfully blind can see it staring him in the face. The endless stoppages in the shipyards and on the waterfronts of Britain, America, and

Australia; the infiltration of Communist leadership into trade unions (only made possible by the ignorance and apathy of the vast majority of decent, loyal trade unionists); constant unofficial strikes organized by Communist and fellow-traveling agitators among shop stewards, all aimed at the paralysis of the trade by which we live; the moronic vaporings of *The Daily Worker* and the scarcely less dangerously subversive, sex-ridden poppycock that is the stock-in-trade of more widely read organs of the press; the muddled busybodiness of well-meaning and sincere, but ignorant, dupes in socialist parties and in movements like the Campaign for Nuclear Disarmament (and equivalent organizations in America): all these (whether those responsible know it or not, and too often they don't) are only a few manifestations of the pattern of Communist "termitry," sapping operations by the Muscovite vanguard of peaceful coexistence.

"It is important for all nations to realize," said a member of the British Cabinet in a recent speech,* "that Communism is a one-way street. So long as freedom persists, the right to vote, the right to free expression, the right to strike, the right to demonstrate are all ruthlessly exploited in the interests of subversion; and military aid, arms, money, and even foreign troops are ruthlessly used in order to install a revolutionary government.

"When, however, the trap has snapped on some unfortunate people, the whole apparatus of military dictatorship is used to hold it down; but should any power from outside, or any exile, or any international movement attempt to give any aid or comfort to the oppressed or any encouragement to opposition—or even assistance to escape—this is immediately labeled as 'aggression,' and the whole doctrine of international law, with its principle of the sovereignty of in-

---

* Lord Hailsham, opening an Atlantic Round Table Conference in London on January 31, 1961.

dependent states, is invoked to keep the victims in subjection. It follows that the best way of meeting Communism is to keep it out."

But it is not only in Europe—indeed, it is not primarily in Europe—that we have to meet the brunt of the Communist offensive foreshadowed in the Moscow declaration. No one can claim that the tragic history of the Congo since July, 1960, is free from mistakes by the United Nations and some Western powers—and notably by Belgium, which is so largely responsible for the tragedy by its craven and grossly premature surrender of power to a lot of semisavages, to whom it had previously given none of the training or experience needed for the exercise of independence. But it is easy enough to criticize from the circle the actions of those involved in the bloody dust of the bull ring. This much, however, can be said: For sheer unadulterated wickedness, it would be hard to beat the record of the Russians and their stooges in the Congo. They are doing their disgraceful utmost to wreck the machinery and authority of the United Nations, acting locally, as usual, by proxy, working through indigenous Moscow-trained extremists, as well as through dupes among the so-called "uncommitted neutrals" who have provided contingents for the U.N. forces; putting up Zorin in the Assembly, with the able support of Krishna Menon, to vilify Western motives and to paralyze Western moves to strengthen the hand of Mr. Dayal in Leopoldville.

The events in the Congo, as well as those in Laos, represent the pattern of things to come. These are the tactics we have to counter, tactics that we have seen and can now see being used actively, tirelessly, and very dangerously—not open, shooting warfare, but the tactics of the termite: the big lie endlessly repeated, the ceaseless flood of vitriolic abuse in a score of languages over Moscow, Peking, and Cairo radios, heard by illiterate millions in thousands of mud villages; infiltration, subversion, and corruption, the use of indigenous traitors and imported agitators; the exploitation of poverty, disease, and ignorance and of the grossly venal and inefficient administration that characterize so many of the new nations; the whipping up by Communist agents of the undisciplined irresponsibility of excitable mobs, often composed of so-called "students" who can always be counted upon to make a nuisance of themselves in the streets instead of in their classrooms; the supplying of arms to anyone who can be trusted to use them irresponsibly; the ceaseless accusation of "colonial imperialism" by the power with the most oppressive colonial record in history.

Whenever and wherever humanly possible, the Communists fish in troubled waters, working ceaselessly and relentlessly to exploit our difficulties where they exist and create them where they do not. Tension in Berlin, irredentism in Cyprus, venal misrule in Cuba, the Arab-Israel impasse, Nasser's hatred of Jordan, the fantastic Indonesian claim to Dutch New Guinea, the Kashmir imbroglio, the revolt in Algeria, the premature pressure for self-government in British Africa, racial tensions in New Orleans—all are grist to the Communist mill. The pattern is always the same: support for any person or any cause as long as it can embarrass the West, and all this going on just as actively whether Khrushchev at the time is kissing American babies in Minnesota or snarling at American journalists in Paris.

The major issue in this second half of the twentieth century is thus the struggle for the hearts and minds of men in our own and other Western countries, and, more particularly, of the yet uncommitted millions in the underdeveloped emergent nations of Asia and Africa. What we are up against in the next stage of the Cold War is not only intense economic and social competition—both of which are good if we understand the situation and meet it wisely and with properly enlightened self-interest—but also what can best be identified by that much-abused term "psychological warfare."

While the Kremlin certainly has a clearly defined aim and a consistent long-term policy to attain it, I am not one of those who believe that every one of their actions is a carefully considered tactical move in a vast, subtle, sinister game of chess. I think they often do things out of sheer stupidity or doctrinaire wrong-headedness which do their own cause more harm than good. They have carried the habitual falsification of truth to a point where they seem sometimes to muddle and confuse themselves as much as other people. They are by no means always clear thinkers, and they have a habit of grossly oversimplifying the most appallingly complex problems. And it is important to realize that, though the man in the Kremlin uses the same words as we do, to him they mean something quite different. He thinks quite differently; one has only to look at the Communist use of the terms "peace-loving" and "people's democracy." A classic example occurred during the arguments in Paris over the U-2 incident, when someone suggested that, after all, the Russians also sometimes engaged in a bit of espionage of their own; Khrushchev raised his hands to heaven and declared passionately, "As God is my witness, my heart is pure, and my hands are clean." The worst of it is that no doubt he really meant it; he thinks that way. When a Russian does something in the Communist interest, it is pure and clean and absolutely justifiable (since it advances the cause of Communism); when someone from the West does the same thing in his own nation's or NATO's interest, it is immoral and criminal, typical of imperialist aggression.

All that having been said, we may as well admit that we have something to learn from the Kremlin in the field of psychological warfare—more to help us counter their attacks, rather than to copy their tactics. And we should at least be aware of the Pavlovian technique because it is taken seriously by the Russians and may well explain much of their international behavior which we find difficult to understand and which, indeed, has gained for them victories in the psychological field that we would do well not to underestimate.

Very briefly, Pavlov's theory and practice, in the words of Dr. William Sargant,* is that "one of the surest ways of breaking down the nervous stability of the dog and of other animals, and producing in them states of uncontrolled neurotic excitement which may later lead on to hysterical and submissive behavior and finally even to depressive apathy [a description, be it noted, that can rather aptly be applied to the state of mind of many adherents to the dogma of unilateral disarmament] is to give a trained, cooperative, but anxious animal a random series of positive and negative conditioned stimuli or signals. A hungry, tense animal, for instance, which has been used to an orderly laboratory existence, in which certain given signals are followed by food and others by no food, can quickly become neurotic and confused when he tries to sort out a sequence of positive and negative food signals, followed indiscriminately by food or no food, which do not and were never intended to make sense to him from the beginning."

It can reasonably be argued that the Kremlin's use of this technique has been as effective in keeping its own people confused and subservient as for any other purpose. But a moment's consideration will confirm that—whether consciously or otherwise, and it is not unreasonable to assume the former —the technique has been used with substantial effect on a number of occasions in the international arena. Recent obvious examples were the conflicting propaganda put out about the first Sputnik and Khrushchev's behavior in Paris over the U-2 incident. Of the latter, one example of its effect was a letter to *The Times* (London) by a Socialist M.P. implying

---

* Member of the Department of Psychological Medicine, St. Thomas Hospital, and author of the book *The Battle for the Mind.*

that the collapse of the summit talks was entirely the fault of the Americans and that Khrushchev's attitude was quite reasonable—even though he had known for years that these espionage flights were going on, but chose to make this particular one the occasion for wrecking the summit conference at the eleventh hour. Another, more recent example of this technique is found in Khrushchev's belligerent Moscow speech, coinciding with his amiable message to Mr. Kennedy.

A grave weakness of this technique, however, is that it depends for success upon the willing cooperation of the victim: "Pavlov could not break down dogs who took no notice at all of all the experimental flashing lights provided for their undoing." But it really is not good enough to assume that this cooperation will never be forthcoming, or to take the complacent line that propaganda is not much of a menace anyway. It is true that Khrushchev's alternations between the roles of jolly little man and strident rocket-rattler, between kissing American babies and slamming desk tops in the U.N. Assembly, left the more mature members of the Western Alliance on the whole surprisingly (and, no doubt, disappointingly) unrattled. But Dr. Sargant's prescription for dealing with this sort of thing—"to deliberately ignore the signals and stop trying to make any sense out of them"—has its limitations. If he means that our governments should not allow it to divert them one inch from the fearless pursuit of our own object in international policy, then, of course, he is right. But it would be unwise to ignore them, if only because to follow them and analyze them carefully may sometimes provide a useful gauge of what the Kremlin really has in mind. We should, as Mr. Macmillan said, take note objectively and dispassionately of these conflicting signals and not underrate their dangerous potentialities. The technique may not have been very effective against NATO nations, but is that true of others—of Japan, for example? Is it, in fact, possible in a free country with an uncontrolled press and radio to ignore these signals? Most of us no doubt have the moral fiber to resist this form of conditioning. But are we so sure that even in Britain and America the technique has paid *no* dividends in the form of what Dr. Sargant describes as "inevitable disturbances of judgment, the increase in hysterical suggestibility"? Might there not be some justification for a claim by the psychological warfare department of the Kremlin to having reduced Her Majesty's official Opposition (we hope only temporarily) to a state of abject impotence, and to having won over an important majority of British trade-union leadership to the cause of unilateral disarmament and the abandonment of NATO? If this were carried to the point—and it is not really that much further—where it became the policy of a future British government, that would be a victory for Communism worth far more than fifty divisions or hydrogen bombs.*

No one in his right mind would accuse men like Bertrand Russell, Canon Collins, or the British labor leader Frank Cousins of being conscious agents of Communism, but the simple fact is that, no doubt unconsciously, they are playing into the hands of the Communists. I know that if a man cannot change his mind, it probably means he doesn't have a mind to change. But, in view of the Pavlovian technique, what is one to think of a world-famous philosopher who in 1957 could say in a newspaper interview about the H-bomb, "I am not in favor of its abolition as I have so often been assumed to be . . . the H-bomb is a real deterrent . . . the only thing that puts East and West on an equal footing"†—and then within three years has set himself up as a sort of

---

* Since this was written, there have been encouraging signs of a return to sanity on the subject of unilateralism in British trade unions and the Labour Party.

† See also Lord Russell's attitude on this subject in *The Bomb* (London: B. T. Batsford, 1955).

antinuclear Gandhi, heading a campaign of civil disobedience designed to force his government into doing the exact thing that the Kremlin would, above all, wish it to do?

The really important point to understand is that this sort of psychological offensive against us can have no effect without active help from inside our own countries. There must be the willing dogs to cooperate in the experiments—and alas, how many and how willing they are; the fact that their cooperation is unwitting makes it no less dangerously effective. They create and hand over freely, as a gift, publicity for which the Communists would gladly pay millions.

One day, the first Sputnik bursts upon the headlines of the West; the next week, we are assured by the self-appointed "experts" of the popular press that the Russians have developed an intercontinental missile; and within a month, the Soviet Union is years ahead of us in rocket techniques. Khrushchev has only to raise his voice, and a newspaper runs in three-inch headlines the news that "Mr. K. Says NO." The word "crisis" is used in each and every unimportant context; fortunately, it has been overworked to such an extent that many people now take no notice of it, but this also poses the traditional danger of the too-oft-repeated cry of "wolf." It is, I suppose, too much to expect a sense of political responsibility on the part of mass-circulation organs whose proprietors are more concerned with lining their pockets through increased circulation than with any other consideration. But at least responsible, serious-minded people who have some influence in the formulation and guidance of public opinion should be aware of the nature and tactics of the enemy in this war of nerves and do what can be done (and there is something) to prevent their less well-informed fellow citizens from playing the enemy's game at every turn.

Some of us have long advocated that some form of psychological-warfare staff make a continuous professional study of Soviet techniques and the means of countering them. The latter, from our point of view, is more important—and far less difficult—than indulging in them ourselves. Let us at least know what the enemy is up to in this area, which at present we do not know—or not nearly enough. I do not advocate a NATO political-warfare executive, with all the Parkinsonian panoply of secretaries and permanent officials. For the most part, the work can best—indeed, can probably only—be done in individual national capitals. There cannot be a common NATO direction of the details; there could and should be a common policy along the broad lines of approach: what effect we want to achieve, and how we want to go about it. And there must be some coordinating clearing house to ensure that our offensive psychological operations at least do not conflict with and contradict each other, but pursue a common goal, and that we also follow a consistent defensive pattern and keep each other and our peoples supplied with the relevant information that each of us obtains through his own channels. The obvious center for such a clearing house is the headquarters of NATO.

Before leaving this brief study of some characteristics of our enemy, I must refer to one further point that emerges clearly from the Moscow declaration, the point that has attracted most public attention in the West: the conclusion that war is not inevitable, not an indispensable stage in the achievement of the Communist aim of world domination. The truth is that the Russians *are* afraid of war. We should not blame them for that; it is one of the few sentiments that the Kremlin shares with normal civilized governments. The inference I want to emphasize is that the too common assumption that we, the democracies, are the only people who shrink from the ultimate option of war is baseless. It is of absolutely cardinal importance for us to understand that.

The Russians would fight, and fight extremely well—would even be prepared to pull the entire world down about them in a thermonuclear holocaust—if Russia itself were attacked or directly threatened. That is not a Communist but a Russian characteristic, as we saw in Hitler's war. We must remember that they are Russians as well as Communists. Many manifestations of their policy contain elements that have remained unchanged since 1917; Russia is "holy Russia" to the Communists, just as it was in the old Czarist creed. It is an admirable characteristic, and it should be understood and respected; it is, indeed, perhaps the only Russian characteristic that we should be sure of emulating.

They will never be attacked or directly threatened from across their Western frontiers. Whether that will be true, in the not very remote future, of the Chinese colossus across their eastern marches is a very different matter that, despite their reiterated lip service to "invincible solidarity," obviously causes them legitimate anxiety. But short of such an attack, the Kremlin has not the remotest intention of risking involvement in total war. It is extremely doubtful that it ever had any such intention, even in the lean days of the late 1940's, when the only material obstacle to easy conquest of Europe was a crude and relatively insignificant American atomic capacity. There was a time after the death of Stalin when it looked as though preventive or pre-emptive war might have a place in Russian strategic thinking; we heard at that time some nonsensical talk about a nuclear war being lethal for capitalism, but not for Communism. We hear no more of that today. The Moscow manifesto speaks of a third world war as "an even more terrible catastrophe . . . the abyss of calamities and horrors of a new world war . . . a global thermonuclear disaster" to be prevented, not to be allowed to break out. It is true that these warnings are embedded in the usual morass of typical Communist verbiage: the possibility of these disasters arises from the aggressive machinations of American, British, and French imperialists and West German *revanchists*, and must be averted by the noble efforts of the peace-loving peoples in the socialist camp. But this, I am confident, is not just another manifestation of Pavlovian technique; it is a genuine policy to which by now the Kremlin is too deeply committed—to its own people as much as to the outside world —to permit any tactical reversal.

Military commentators in the Soviet Union are not independent critics as they are in Britain and America; they would get short shrift if, like their opposite numbers in the free world, they were to publish views not in accordance with the policy of their government. Listen to General Talensky, the most influential exponent of Soviet military thought, writing in October, 1960, in the Russian journal *International Affairs*. In his view, conventional weapons will have only "auxiliary significance" and will be of secondary importance in any future war, which he assumes as a matter of course would be fought with nuclear weapons. "Armed conflict with such weapons," he writes, "will undoubtedly embrace the whole world. No state that enters a war will escape crushing and destructive blows. . . . It will lead to the complete devastation of the territory of almost the whole of Europe and North America. . . ." He goes on to say, "The mortal danger from radioactive fallout endangers not only the peoples of the belligerent countries, but the whole population of our planet. . . . The population of the world would be reduced by half, and in addition it would be the most active, competent, and civilized part of humanity that would perish." Finally, and perhaps most significantly, "Human society would be thrown backward and its road to Communism immeasurably lengthened."

That all this is true no one in the free world is likely to deny. The essential point is that *this is the way the Kremlin thinks;* this is the background to its consideration of international affairs, the yardstick by which it will measure its policy where any risk of war is involved. In view of this, can anyone seriously maintain that the Russians should be taken seriously when they indulge in rocket-rattling about Berlin or Suez or Cuba?

Not only does this attitude toward war result in their sharing with the West certain apprehensions about the spread of nuclear weapons to smaller powers. It also makes them afraid of limited wars—minor conflicts on the Korean model—because they doubt that they could be contained and remain limited. "In modern conditions," writes Talensky, "local and limited wars will be nothing other than a prelude to general nuclear rocket war, one of the ways of unleashing a war." It would be quite wrong to take this merely as a threat, though no doubt that is how the Kremlin would like it to be taken. It is the expression of a genuine apprehension.

I stress this factor of the Soviet Union's genuine and perfectly understandable dread of modern war because I believe it to be an indispensable background to what follows. It must be borne in mind as an important factor and applied as a yardstick to measure Russian intentions when considering each of the recommendations for action contained in the ensuing chapters of this book. Properly understood, it lends to the pursuit of our policy that flexibility and freedom of action —within the bounds of decent caution, far short of brinkmanship, but also free from timidity—which is essential if we are to hold our own against the grosser forms of peaceful coexistence with which the Communists will undoubtedly face us in the coming years.

Chapter 3

Some Basic Principles

The best way of meeting
Communism is to keep it out.

(LORD HAILSHAM)

IF WHAT I HAVE thus far outlined is accepted as a fair indication of the nature, scope, and tempo of the threat with which
we are faced, the next thing to consider is what to do about it.
Before going on to submit certain practical proposals and suggest some limited objectives for our strategy, it seems desirable
to sketch in a background of certain more general considerations, some broad principles on which I think our policy
should be based in countering Communist action and winning
the Cold War in Britain, North America, and Europe and in
the wider spheres of Asia, Africa, and Latin America.

It should first be said that to adopt a tough realistic attitude
to the global Communist menace does not mean that we
should relax for a moment our efforts to bridge the chasms
that divide the world. We must always be on the alert to
identify and respond to any genuine modification of Communist policy. As long as the Russians want to be our enemies,
then our enemies they shall be; if and when they want to become our friends, we will be only too happy to accept and

treat them as such. But it must be real friendship, not the tactic of the Trojan horse. And here, as in everything, we must take the initiative; we must not be content merely with defense and counterattack against cold aggression, but must seek tirelessly to change the attitude of mind that directs it. Unconditional surrender makes no more sense in this Cold War than it did in the last hot one; we must always be ready for some give and take, to go out to meet them if they show any signs of coming to meet us—but always with the proviso that we do not do it at the expense of other peoples or compromise with principles upon which our freedom and way of life depend. Despite the December manifesto, I do not consider such a quest quite so hopeless as is commonly supposed.

We rightly resent the declared intention of the Communists to destroy what they so absurdly call "capitalism," and do not propose to allow them to do anything of the kind. We must recognize, however regretfully, that this is a two-way street. However much we may dislike and despise the Communist political system, with all its paraphernalia of the police state and its suppression of human freedoms, we have no divinely appointed mission—as Mr. Dulles sometimes seemed to think—to liberate the satellite states and destroy Communism as a system of government. However much we might like to, we cannot be our brother's keeper to that extent. We should do everything possible within the bounds of practical realism to change the minds of the Communist rulers, working both directly and through their peoples as far as we can: by well-directed and adult forms of propaganda, remembering the truth we learned in the last war, that to encourage subject peoples to revolt is worse than useless unless we can support them quickly by military action, which of course, as a general rule, is manifestly out of the question in the present case; by never allowing a Communist lie to go unanswered (a full-time job in itself!); by East-West trade; by everything that comes under the general heading of cultural relations, including especially the encouragement of tourist travel and the exchange of visits by specialists, students, and young people—an activity that, in our own countries, should be sponsored by loyal, respectable institutions instead of by the fellow-traveling, crypto-Communist bodies too often prominent in this field; and by negotiating with the Communist rulers and representatives and holding our own with them in the many international organizations, particularly the United Nations and its specialized agencies.

But I'm afraid that we must accept with regret the reality that there is, in fact, no rapid or spectacular action open to us whereby we can change the system of government in Russia and other Communist states. If their peoples change it themselves in due course, well and good—and few people in the West will shed a tear if some heads roll in the process. It may sound unambitious, but I am sure the only hope in this area—and it is one that I think we may look forward with some confidence to seeing fulfilled within the next generation—is the gradual evolution of Communism into something more reasonable and civilized, a development we should certainly encourage in every possible way. And however prosaic it may seem, the first way to set about doing that is to put our own houses in order and present an example of wise, firm, but patient policy, proving beyond doubt to friends and enemies alike that the free way of life is in every way superior to Communism.

I know that this is the sort of boring statement constantly made on political platforms; but it is nonetheless true. And I don't think we need be pessimistic about the prospects for a radical change in the practice of Communism, if perhaps not in its theory. After all, as a political philosophy, it is what has been described as a "Victorian anachronism"; it had some basis of reason and justice in the social conditions prevailing in the nineteenth century, when Marx wrote the *Communist Manifesto*, but it makes no sense in the entirely changed conditions of today. One must admit that under it, or in spite of it, Russian achievements during the past forty-odd years have been immense. It is true that they have been made at a terrible cost in human life, suffering, and freedom; and we might have seen them come about under a continuing Czarist regime, though it is only fair to admit that that seems doubtful. But those very achievements probably contain within themselves the seeds of Communism's decay. It was all very well for Stalin and the old Bolsheviks to impose by force their brutal regime upon a predominantly illiterate nation of moujiks and freed serfs who had just thrown off the yoke of an inefficient feudal despotism in a grossly underdeveloped country. It is quite another thing to continue to impose that system upon a largely literate, educated, intelligent population like that of the Soviet Union today.

It is important to realize that not only the masses but also the intelligentsia—the prosperous, middle-class, professional people in Russia—have almost all been brought up with knowledge about no other system besides Communism. The background of their thinking is Communist in the same way, and probably to about the same degree, as the background of our thinking in the West is Christian; and much that they see at home and abroad testifies in their eyes to the superior virtues of Communism. Most of them have no means of comparing the achievements of capitalism; they are not allowed to know, and are, in fact, fantastically misinformed about, what goes on in other countries. It is vain to imagine that there is any possibility of violent overthrow of the Soviet regime. But it is difficult to believe that the Russian people of today and tomorrow, as it becomes increasingly difficult to keep them in ignorance (and this is bound to happen), will long continue to put up with the crass absurdities and glaring injustices that characterize the Communist governmental system, the suppression of truth and glorification of falsehood, the almost pathological fear of the results of any contact with the outside world, and the blatant contradictions and dangers of what stands for Soviet foreign policy.

One hears people in the West talking fearfully about the scope and tempo of scientific education in the Soviet Union; surely we ought to welcome it and do all we can to help it. Science knows no frontiers; and it may not be too much to hope that it will be the scientist, bearing as he does such a terrible responsibility for the most ghastly instruments of man's destruction, who will yet emerge as the prime architect of the bridge between the peoples of Russia and the West.

All this should not be taken to mean that we should adopt a purely negative attitude, using the "great deterrent" as a Maginot Line behind which we sit waiting for the leopard to change his spots, eagerly scanning the horizon for the cloud no larger than a man's hand which may mean that the Communist bosses are at last prepared to meet us and be reasonable about this or that. On the contrary, our urgent need is to regain the initiative and subject the Russians to every possible pressure to change their policies—not merely to remain on the defensive, but to launch an active political offensive.

To some tidy minds, there may appear to be a contradiction here: If it is not for us to intervene to help the people of country A change their system of government *from* Communism, why should we intervene to help the people of country B resist changing their system of government *to* Communism. But this again is a two-way street—or should be. "The best way of meeting Communism is to keep it out." It depends, of course, to some extent on what we mean by intervention. I am not suggesting that a British force should enter Baghdad to prevent General Kassem from being supplanted by Colonel Mahdawi, or that the United States should invade Cuba to overthrow Fidel Castro. Nor do I suggest—as will be made clear later—that we should never use force. But do not let us be too logical or legalistic; logic carried to extremes is liable to lead to lunacy—or slavery. If your enemy insists on all-out wrestling, it is no good trying to compete under Queensberry rules. "The world Communist movement," to quote Lord Hailsham again, "is disclosed as a single conspiracy by a self-confessed dictatorship operating through individual parties centrally controlled . . . and coordinated under the leadership of the Communist Party of Soviet Russia. This is the mechanism of Communist imperialism, and it is the most serious threat to human liberty that has ever existed." Let us by all means be liberal where and when it makes sense—as it very often does; let us be as "reactionary" as Lord Palmerston or Theodore Roosevelt where our very existence is at stake. "There is nothing more easy to subvert than democratic processes."* There is nothing less easy to subvert in a Communist-controlled country than Communist processes. Even if one gets through the physical Iron Curtain of barbed wire and frontier guards, and the intellectual Iron Curtain of jammed radios and a controlled press, the internal system of secret police and mutual espionage is infinitely more difficult to penetrate than the free and easy, fully informed, open society of the West.

We are, at best, terribly handicapped in this sort of warfare—and if I have not convinced my readers by now that it *is* warfare, I have already failed in my purpose. Termitry is a powerful offensive weapon in the hands of the Communists; it is always easier to undermine existing institutions than to protect them. And for a variety of obvious reasons, it is impossible for us in our counteroffensive—even if it were desirable—to adopt all the tactics of the termite. But at least we should not intensify our disadvantage by making things too easy for—and even extending gratuitous assistance to—Communist subversion in the free countries. We must be really

---

* William Carron, of the Amalgamated Engineering Union, in a television broadcast.

tough in our own defense, stopping short only at measures that would in themselves distort and subvert the true character of our free institutions. And in overseas activities, let us not handicap ourselves unduly by a too rigorous adherence to the rules of the game as we see them. This is not a game. There are, for instance, occasions when the golden bullet is much more effective—and cheaper in the long run—than the lead one; I have known occasions on which we could have used it to good effect had we not thought it beneath our dignity to do so. Let us not be ridden with guilt complexes or handicapped by the "old school tie." Let us, at least in defense, be as uncompromising to protect our free democratic system in our own and in the uncommitted countries as the Communists are to perpetuate their domination within their orbit. Can anyone imagine the Kremlin tolerating in Russia or, say, in Lithuania or Uzbekistan actions by the West of the kind that we sit anxiously by and see occurring under our noses at home and in, say, Egypt or the Yemen?

For some reason, the old conception of spheres of interest seems to have acquired an aura of disreputable Victorianism. But why? As a concept, it represents one of the facts of life. We should say to the Russians, in effect—"We realize you have a sphere of interest. You must acknowledge the same to us. We dislike your methods, but they are your affair, and we don't intend to butt in on your bailiwick. The same applies to you. We don't intend to tolerate your infiltrations, to allow the foundations of our spheres of interest to be gnawed away by your termites. You are as entitled as we are to legitimate trade anywhere you can find it; we welcome your taking a share in the economic buildup of underdeveloped countries. We do *not* intend to allow you to impose Communism either overtly or covertly by foul means in countries within our spheres of interest, and we give you fair warning that, if you try, you will find us your enemy and we will meet you with your own weapons." I may be wrong, but I have a feeling that that is the sort of language the Russian understands.

We should not define our spheres of interest; the Kremlin leaders will know well enough, and if they are uncertain, there are plenty of ways of letting them know. We should never specify in advance what used to be called a "stop line" —no "thus far and no farther"; that merely serves as a green light for intervention short of the stop line and automatically throws anyone on the far side of it into the Communist orbit. We certainly should not openly disclaim interest in any specific area, as the United States did in Korea, thus inviting the Korean aggression. We should keep our enemy guessing, as long as we don't at the same time keep our allies guessing. But when the specific occasion arises, we should be prompt with our warning—and issue it quietly, through the established diplomatic channels that exist for the purpose. It is always wise on these occasions to give your adversary the opportunity to back down without losing face.

In an earlier book,* I expressed the view that any pacts or treaties with the Communists "should as far as possible not be dependent for their validity upon Communist good faith—that is, they should be of the nature of formal clarifications of intention in given circumstances." We can sometimes make a start in the direction we want to take—give an initial impetus to the stream that may ultimately wash away a log jam (as I will suggest later in connection with arms control)—by unilateral action, presenting our opponents with a *fait accompli* that involves no unacceptable risk to ourselves, without having to waste interminable months or perhaps exacerbating differences by engaging in tedious dialectics with such specialists at that game as Zorin.

---

* *Strategy for the West* (London: Cassell & Co., 1954; New York: William Morrow, 1954).

We have, incidentally, some reason to be thankful that the new U.S. Administration appears to take a more practical and realistic view of the mythical virtues of so-called "summit talks."* There is obviously everything to be said for the leaders of the free world consulting each other personally and privately, accompanied by their responsible advisers, to coordinate their policies at the highest level. To simple people, there is a mystical—and, I suppose, up to a point natural—appeal in the idea, originally put forth by Winston Churchill (who should have known better), of the top men on both sides getting together and ironing it all out in face-to-face meetings; and the urge has sometimes been difficult to resist for electoral reasons in the democracies (another of our disadvantages, as compared with the Communists). The underlying fallacy, of course, is the idea that the other side has any desire to "iron it all out"; on the contrary (as the December declaration should, but probably won't, make clear to most of us), there is nothing further from their intentions. We should by now be educated to understand that top-level public diplomacy by Presidents and Prime Ministers with a man like Khrushchev, under the glare of the TV cameras and the eyes of a thousand journalists, is simply courting trouble; it means not "open agreements openly arrived at" (that asinine phrase), but in the long run open disagreements openly exacerbated. If we imagine that the sort of good-fellowship, college-fraternity conception exemplified by the "spirit of Camp David" means anything whatever to a ruthless dictator like Khrushchev except an instrument to be used for his own ends, we are asking for the sort of defeat that we suffered at the abortive Paris summit meeting. This may be wisdom through hindsight, but it is better to be wise after the last event than silly before the next one.

---

* See Dean Rusk, "The President," *Foreign Affairs*, April, 1960; and Henry Kissinger, "The Next Summit Meeting," *Harper's Magazine*, December, 1960.

This does not mean we should never negotiate with the Communists; far from it, we should take every opportunity of trying to reach reasonable agreements with them, provided we do it with our eyes open. But we must be quite clear about what negotiation means to them. Let me quote from an earlier book: "To us in the West it suggests a meeting between two parties each of whom has at least some ideas in common as to the sort of result they want to achieve; who are genuinely prepared to compromise, to the extent of some degree of give and take; who accept that it will be in the wider interest of both to honor the result of the negotiation, even if it involves some sacrifice or inconvenience to themselves—and who both attach the same meaning to words."* On this sort of basis, some useful results have been known to flow from discussion on lower levels—for instance, in scientific and technical fields —between Western and Russian specialists. Not so in the spheres of higher policy. The Communist leader regards negotiation first as a means of getting what he wants, of gaining advantage for himself at the expense of others, and secondly as an instrument of propaganda. There is nothing wrong with propaganda as long as it is truthful and not just obviously self-serving; but it is to be condemned when it is used as a weapon, as Communist propaganda always is—blatantly dishonest, rooted in lies, designed only to confuse, to divide and mislead, appealing to the ignorance of the simple, the prejudices of the misguided, or the natural emotions of ordinary decent people (and usually all three).

An excellent example of the Communist idea of negotiation was Khrushchev's proposal of September, 1959, for general and complete disarmament, leaving only police and gendarmerie, within four years. That proposal was in one sense an instance of the Russian habit of grossly oversimplifying very complicated subjects—no doubt partly caused by the fact that they had not then (and, indeed, still have not) really

_____
* *Strategy for the West.*

considered the issue as thoroughly as we have in the West. But Khrushchev himself is not such a fool as to have imagined that his plan was really practicable or stood the slightest chance of acceptance by anyone—least of all, perhaps, by his friends in Peking. It was, however, a marvelous propaganda point, with tremendous appeal to the simple and uninformed. It sounds so obvious and satisfying: Eliminate all armed forces so that we are "no longer able to wage war"—just like that! It was beautifully calculated to find ready acceptance, not only by the well-meaning but unrealistic sentimentalists in our own countries, but still more by the new and politically immature nations who have no responsibilities (and, incidentally, few arms to discard) and who find it so easy and apparently enjoyable to give moral lectures to their more powerful partners in the United Nations, knowing that they themselves will not be personally affected.

But it was also (and this is the point here) a typical example of the Russian attitude toward negotiation. In all past disarmament negotiations, we on the Western side have always insisted on the need for a military balance during the process of disarmament by stages. The Russians, while paying some lip service to this principle, always treat such negotiations as a method of gaining military advantage for themselves. Nothing could suit the Russian politico-strategic purpose better than the acceptance of this idea of a complete disarming to the level of only those forces necessary for internal security. Not only would it release the Soviet manpower urgently required for other purposes—agriculture, the virgin lands, heavy industry, housing, increased production of consumer goods, and so on; this is a perfectly legitimate aim that has much in common with our own desires. But also, for the Russians, it would result in the complete security of their own country from external attack; the abolition of any deterrent to their ambitions, laying open the Continent to domination by Russian "internal security" troops (as there could be no

effective check on the strength of these forces); and free rein
for Communist termite tactics in the rest of the world. And
it would make it impossible for the United States, Britain,
or France to defend themselves, their interests or their friends,
in Europe or anywhere else.

In short, Khrushchev's proposal represented a perfectly
logical extension, though in a dramatically new form, of the
Russians' traditional technique in which their disarmament
plans form an integral component of their strategic policy—
the object being, as always, to gain a military advantage
for Communism.

So when we sit down to negotiation with Communists, let
us be on our guard and make no concessions whatever that
are not compensated for by equivalent and verifiable concessions on the Communist side. When any development of
policy is under discussion that contains any risks or disadvantages to our side, we must consider first whether they are
any greater than those involved in the indefinite continuation
of the status quo, wherever it may be, and then refuse to go
any further with the negotiations unless any new risks or disadvantages for ourselves are at least matched by equivalent
risks and disadvantages for our opponents.

The Russians are quite capable of understanding that. As
I have already pointed out, they themselves will never agree
to anything reasonable (as we understand the word) unless
they believe the result to be, on balance, advantageous to
them, despite its compensating advantages for us. They will
not accept anything that they think will do more than delay
the ultimate triumph of Communism. We should not worry
unduly about that; time is not necessarily on our side, but
neither is it against us unless we fail to make proper use of it.
We simply should not expect too much of negotiations with
the Russians, and we should not aim too high.

What we have to do is identify points or areas of common

interest—matters on which there is reason to believe that agreement may suit the Kremlin as much as it suits us. There are some; and it is my aim here to examine those that seem to me to emerge either from the Moscow declaration or from other current evidence of Russian intentions or fears—and to suggest that it will contribute to the attainment of our aim to adopt policies that accord with them. I have already suggested what some of these areas of mutual interest may be, and later on, I will enlarge on the ways of exploiting them. But to clarify my theme, I will list them here:

1) The Russians dread total war, being convinced that it would mean global nuclear catastrophe and mutual suicide.

2) They wish to avoid limited war, such as the one we experienced in Korea, because they believe it could not be kept limited, but would lead to total war.

3) On the other hand—and here is one area in which we do not share a common interest—they do not exclude from their program what they are pleased to call "wars of national liberation," i.e., rebellion in colonial and other less stable countries (among which Khrushchev, in his January, 1961, speech specifically included Algeria and Indochina). In this sort of war, it is regarded as a sacred duty of Communism to help the "oppressed peoples." (It is essential to the theme of this book that the Communist attitude toward these three different kinds of war should be clearly understood.)

4) They are worried about what is known as the "Nth-power" problem, the spread of nuclear weapons among a wider circle of powers. They are anything but anxious to see their satellites thus armed—to say nothing of Red China, though they probably realize that in the long run there is nothing they can do to prevent the Chinese from acquiring nuclear weapons on their own.

5) They have a genuine and historically justified fear of surprise attack. Largely because of their own almost psychopathic obsession for secrecy, the fact that they suffered far

more terribly in World War II at the hands of the Germans than did any of their allies is not widely enough appreciated. And if the Americans are haunted to some degree by a Pearl Harbor complex (the extent and influence of which we actually tend to exaggerate), the Russians have infinitely more cogent grounds for such anxiety. In 1941, when their Nazi accomplices of 1939 launched about 100 divisions in a surprise attack against them, they were subjected to appalling devastation and losses. The fact that they need not have been thus surprised if they had heeded our warning is beside the point now.

6) Offensive war—the traditional kind of shooting war— cannot be considered an instrument of their policy, as it has been of other nations in the past. Their record is replete with examples of absorption by force or by the threat of force of weaker states beyond their own frontiers—the Central European satellites being the primary example. But no great war has started with the invasion by Russia of a neighboring major country, as several have been by Germany and France. On the other hand, Russian history is full of invasions by foreign armies—Mongols, Swedes, Poles, French, Germans, even the British in a minor, bungling, rather absent-minded way. So it is not altogether unreasonable for the Russians to regard the European satellites as a defensive glacis, originally occupied in the course of a counteroffensive in a war of defense initiated by the German invasion of Russia. It is true that for centuries they have been gradually advancing or trying to advance their frontiers by infiltration and erosion of adjacent soft spots—in Central Asia, in Manchuria, in Persia, in the Balkans, in the Indian borderlands. But a characteristic of their policy, common to both the Communist and the Czarist empires, has been the tactical withdrawal in the face of determined opposition. That characteristic will surely be enhanced now that the cataclysmic fury of nuclear air power

has annulled the traditional security formerly inherent in the vast, desolate reaches of Russia.

7) The Russians are obviously, and very naturally, nervous about Red China. They probably do not anticipate, at least in the near future, actual invasion across their Central Asian frontier; but they do fear the prospect of finding themselves embroiled in a war against the Western powers arising from some rashly impetuous action on the part of this neighboring colossus, over whom their control becomes weaker with every year that passes.

8) Finally, for the reasons outlined above, they do genuinely want some measure of disarmament—provided, of course, that it lends advantage to the Communist cause.

Chapter 4

Disarmament – Illusion and Reality

FROM THESE perhaps somewhat rarefied general levels, let us move closer to the particular, though still for a time dealing more with important generalities than with tactical measures to meet specific situations.

We turn first to a feature of our policy that affects our strategy in all fields—at home, in Europe, and beyond— namely, that which is commonly and I think often misleadingly known as "disarmament." I shall not bore the reader with a reiteration or analysis of the weary series of abortive negotiations in recent years.* I am concerned here with examining various aspects of the subject only in relation to our policy for the next decade or so aimed at achieving ultimately the object set forth in the first chapter.

Actually, it is better wherever possible to avoid using the

---

* For a useful summary of the most recent negotiations and the position at the end of 1960, see *The Search for Disarmament* (London: Her Majesty's Stationery Office, 1960).

term "disarmament" except in its true, specific meaning—that is, the gradual reduction and eventual abolition of armaments —because for the period we are now considering, we cannot hope to see any very dramatic reduction of armaments, and abolition is completely out of the question. A less misleading term to describe what we are going to be concerned with in the near future is "arms control," which has been well defined* as "restraint jointly exercised upon armaments policy, whether in respect of the level of armaments, their character, deployment, or use." Arms control is to be considered not as an alternative to disarmament, as the Communists pretend for propaganda purposes to believe that we regard it, but as a concomitant, a first phase wherein the objective would be to create an atmosphere in which actual disarmament could take shape. Nevertheless, disarmament has now assumed a widely accepted generalized meaning; and it would perhaps be unduly pedantic to confine the use of the term to its narrower and more strictly accurate sense.

At the risk of repeating what is sometimes regarded as a truism, I must begin by emphasizing that armaments are a symptom of international tensions, not the cause. The terrible shadow of the nuclear mushroom cloud may act as a nervous irritant, lending a sharp edge to tensions, but it does not create them. There is no truth in the popular parrot cry that an arms race always leads to war; I know of no war whose real cause was an arms race. Disarmament is neither an end in itself, nor is it really very important—and it is not even as important in the economic sphere as is commonly supposed, on anything but a long-term basis. The popular idea that we have only to throw away our armaments and we shall immediately be able to release vast sums of money for aid to underdeveloped countries is largely fallacious. Few people have any

---

* See Hedley Bull, *The Control of the Arms Race* (The Institute for Strategic Studies; London: Weidenfeld & Nicolson, 1961; New York: Frederick A. Praeger, 1961).

conception, for instance, of the enormous capital and recurring cost of an inspection system—not even for a 100 per cent foolproof one, but for one of the proportions that we would have to insist on for many years to come.

No, the prime object of disarmament is *to stabilize a given political situation and ensure that it can be altered only by negotiation*—by "peaceful change," to use the old term—and not by force. If we were satisfied with the present world situation as a permanent state of affairs and could be sure that our opponents do not want to change it, then we could safely proceed with disarmament at once. But is either of those conditions valid? Obviously not. It should not require the Moscow declaration to make clear that at least the second one is pure wishful thinking. From that, it should follow that before we go any further than a limited measure of arms control, we must be clear in our own minds as to what form we want any peaceful change to take; and disarmament cannot precede, but must go step by step along with, political solutions of the problems that divide the world. In other words, if the object of disarmament is to stabilize a given situation, we clearly defeat that object from the beginning unless we make up our minds, in terms more specific than those set forth in my opening chapter, what the situation is that we want to stabilize.

For this reason, I think that the failure of disarmament negotiations to date—though mainly due to Communist intransigence—is also the result to some degree of an undue concentration on our part upon the technical and procedural aspects of the problem, and a failure to realize that they mean nothing in themselves. Such intricate matters as force levels, the "cutoff" and the storage or disposal of agreed stockpiles of different kinds of weapons, the notification of launchings of missiles and space vehicles, methods of verification of agreement to suspend nuclear tests, the detailed methods of control and inspection, Macmillan's idea of a joint panel of military and scientific experts to tell us *how* to disarm—all these things are important, but not in themselves. It is not only *how* to disarm that matters, but *why* we should disarm. These technical details are positively dangerous if they are not matched by parallel steps in the political field. If any progress is to be made, we must first agree among ourselves, at least in general terms, as to the situations we want to create and stabilize in the various areas of tension—in other words, where we want to go. We must then proceed along that road, by verified stages, with technical and tactical measures of arms control coordinated with measures of mutual political adjustment. And here again, we should follow the strategy of limited objectives —the first staging post on the road in Europe being (as I will outline later in more detail) redeployment of conventional forces and limitation of tactical atomic weapons, along with a measure of German reunification and the defusing of the delayed-action bomb of Berlin.

Let us bear in mind throughout that the deadlock in Europe is primarily a crisis of confidence. Neither side trusts the other a yard—which is not to say that we don't have far more cogent grounds for mistrust of the Kremlin than it does for mistrusting us. An essential condition for any appreciable progress in arms control or toward political solutions is that we should make at least a first step toward eroding the wall of mistrust and suspicion that divides East from West. To that end, a jointly supervised system of control and inspection in a limited area could have a real value. And in that context, there are some grounds for encouragement in the latter stages of the prolonged deliberations of the Three-Power Committee on Nuclear Tests (suspended before the American election in 1960), in which the Russian representative seems to have been less impossible to deal with than most Soviet negotiators. The important point is that this Committee has come reasonably close to agreement on the principles on which a control and inspection system should be organized. These principles could become the basis for wider measures of arms control and inspection; for that reason, we should put every possible pressure on the Russians to reach agreement without further interminable delays. At the moment of writing, there seem to be some grounds for cautious optimism in this regard; if this optimism proves to be justified, it will mean a first faltering step toward the re-establishment of some degree of mutual trust. There will be a long and weary way to go, but it will be a start.*

This brings me to the first of two important general points that must be made about the development of arms control. A feature of all Western disarmament proposals has been insistence on an effective system of control and inspection: disarmament by stages, each carefully controlled and verified. That must remain an absolute condition of any future agreement.

The Russian attitude toward this condition has been typical. The idea of control and inspection arouses not only the almost pathological suspicion that is a national characteristic, but also the Russians' practical awareness that it would weaken their own system of secrecy, which gives them an undoubted military advantage over the West, with its wide-open system. Thus, they first maintained that this condition was just a deliberately obstructive one imposed by the imperialist warmongers, who didn't really want disarmament at all—that we should go ahead and disarm and worry about inspection later, that control and inspection before disarmament amounts merely to espionage. Then there was the proposal for international inspection posts at key points, which they did not think would be a crippling disadvantage to them,

---

* Since this was written, events have proved it to be unduly optimistic. And Khrushchev's insistence on the *troika* system, which would give the Communists a veto power in any negotiation, bodes ill not only for disarmament but for any international agreement in which the Soviet Union is involved.

though they had no intention of accepting Eisenhower's "open skies" plan, which clearly might be. After the propaganda exercise of the 1955 summit, they moved toward an agreement to subject their own air bases to inspection, because that would have given them the military advantage of inspection of the far more numerous and efficient bases of the American Strategic Air Command. Then, as the balance was redressed and their own striking power became relatively more efficient with the advent of the ballistic missile, their attitude hardened. A recent manifestation of this was Khrushchev's statement that with a general and comprehensive disarmament, he would accept any inspection that the United States chose to suggest. His reasoning was obvious: Not only did Khrushchev not believe that his condition would ever be fulfilled, so that it was safe for him to score his propaganda point; but also, if it were, then Allied inspection in Russia on anything but a totally impracticable scale would be ineffective, and Russian inspection in America would be unnecessary. (Indeed, it has always been a bit difficult to understand why the Russians consider it necessary to devote such large resources to their intensive and utterly unscrupulous espionage system; for it would not be much of an exaggeration to say that even now all they need to do is to subscribe to *Time*, *Life*, *Fortune*, and various Western scientific and technical journals.)

Here, as in all aspects of disarmament policy, the Russian aim is to gain military advantage. For this reason, we must remain firm in our position—no effective control and inspection, no disarmament.

At the same time, here again we should be guided by the principle of limited objectives. If we try to go too far too fast we shall run smack into the unscaleable wall of Russian suspicion and secrecy—and thus get nowhere. So let us seek a gradual, less drastic approach. We should concentrate first on what seems likely to be practicable and on what may seem to the Russians to suit them as well as it does us. Let us get some measure of control and inspection in a limited area over a limited measure of arms control; and when that has been tested and proved, then we can go on to the next step. Even a small step in this direction would at least constitute a start toward erosion of the wall of mistrust. If we try to get a comprehensive, watertight scheme at the outset, we shall never make that start.

An added reason for adopting, in this context, a policy of gradualness is that the development of nuclear energy and the accumulation of stockpiles have actually reached a point at which any effective inspection or control is quite impossible. And this brings me to the second general point: in the area of nuclear disarmament (when we have gone that far), our practical objective must be the control and perhaps ultimate abolition of the means of delivery.

I want to try to clarify here what seems to me a vital principle in relation to nuclear disarmament that is widely misunderstood. It is this misunderstanding that is largely responsible for such movements as the Campaign for Nuclear Disarmament in Britain and its equivalent in other countries, and for the emotionalism displayed at the Socialist Conference at Scarborough in 1960, which threw the official Parliamentary Opposition at Westminster into its present disastrous confusion. To expose all the follies of unilateralism would require a book in itself; I shall therefore confine myself to what I believe to be the governing fallacy.

There is much in the sentiments and emotions underlying the urge for nuclear disarmament with which all of us can sympathize. But the one attitude of these unilateral enthusiasts with which I find it difficult to be patient is the implicit—and, indeed, sometimes explicit—assumption that to them alone the light has been vouchsafed, that they alone have grasped the full extent of the horrors of nuclear war, and that only they are completely honest in wishing to lift that curse from mankind.

There could be no more infantile delusion. It is notable that the periodic pilgrimages along the road to Aldermarston include a high proportion of young people, most of whom have had little experience of war, though some may have memories of an austere childhood, dominated by the crash of falling bombs and the tragedies of friends and relatives killed or maimed. The movement does attract numbers of older men and women, and they probably include a higher proportion of cranks, Communists, and fellow travelers than there is among the youth. I suppose it is inevitable and natural, up to a point, that young people should regard men of an older generation as mostly a lot of Blimps and Bourbons who either glorify war for its own sake or whose minds are so atrophied by age and prejudice that they accept war as part of the natural order of things and just hope that it won't happen. But most of these young crusaders are intelligent enough to realize, if they give it any thought, that men who have taken an active part in two world wars might reasonably be expected to be at least as concerned as they to eliminate the possibility of a third. It might also occur to them that this applies even more strongly to those of us whose interest or duty it has been to familiarize ourselves with the realities and potentialities of nuclear warfare.

The fact is, of course, that the aim of every one of us (except, perhaps, an insignificant lunatic fringe that does not count) is the same: to abolish war, nuclear or otherwise. What some of us, whose experience and qualifications to exercise judgment in these matters is perhaps superior to those of our young critics, may understand better than they is that to eliminate nuclear weapons without obviating the underlying causes of war would merely put conventional war back on the map—and further, that in our age another prolonged war (and we should know by now that a conventional world war could not possibly be short) would inevitably see the nuclear weapon back in the picture before it ended. Does not all history prove that it is worse than useless trying to abolish any particular weapon of war?* What we have to abolish is war itself. I have hammered away at the point for some years now (and I think the Moscow declaration amply confirms my view) that modern science *has* abolished war—total war as I have known it twice in my time, and the unthinkable horrors of a future great war—*provided* only that we do not throw away the nuclear weapon prematurely.

The prime and conclusive justification of that weapon is not that it will be used, but that it will *not* be used. Nor, as long as it exists, will any other weapons have to be used in another great war. I have already attempted to explain that the item on the credit side of nuclear armaments—and it is an overwhelming one—is that with them war can never again be profitable by any stretch of the imagination. Do we really want to turn that clock back?

Let me cite one example. I have no sentimental weakness for Germans, having spent some ten years of my life fighting them and having seen scores of my friends killed by them. But the Germany of Adenauer is not the Germany of Bismarck, or of Wilhelm II, or of Hitler. The winds of change have blown through Germany as elsewhere, and the Federal Republic is now our ally. It is as absurd today to cavil at details like training facilities for German troops in our countries as it would have been twenty years ago to refuse to support our Russian ally in Hitler's war, at great cost and

---

* The oft-used analogy of gas is not a true one at all. Gas is in a completely different category from the hydrogen bomb. It was not used in the early stages of World War II because neither side regarded it as a decisive weapon. By the time the Germans had access to the terrible "nerve gas," which might have been decisive, British and American bombers were ranging at will all over their country, and to use it then must have seemed to them clearly suicidal.

loss of life to ourselves, as we did. But, that having been said, is anyone prepared to stake his last penny on the certainty that, in different circumstances, we could never again see a revival of Prussian militarism? (Surely no Russian is—and for understandable reasons.) The Germans know that as long as the nuclear weapon exists, their country is sure to emerge from any future war in Europe as little more than a radio-active charnel house. As long as this is a certainty there is not the remotest chance, in my view, that any future Hitler could stampede his country into aggressive war. Are we all quite sure that this would necessarily remain true if the only weapons on either side were modern versions of the *Panzers* and *Stukas* of 1940? I wonder.

All this is not to say that we can never look forward to the elimination of this portentous instrument of Man's destruction. It may be that the young crusaders of Aldermarston will live to see that day. But if they, and the earnest clerics and clever academics who swell their ranks, succeed in forcing the pace—if the trade-union unilateralists and left-wing extremists ever do succeed in reducing a British Government to nuclear impotence and disintegrating the Atlantic Alliance —then nothing is more certain than that the result would be not the peaceful end of the Cold War but our defeat in it.

The majority of these people are well-meaning and sincere; there are termites among them, but for the most part they are devoted, patriotic, compassionate people who genuinely want to build Jerusalem in England's green and pleasant land. Few, if any, of them will read this book. But if only they would read the Moscow declaration, Khrushchev's speeches, and the articles of Talensky—if they would only mark, learn, and digest the inner meaning of Communist policy—they would realize that the triumph of their present misguided crusade would bring back "Satanic mills" far darker than any in their philosophy.

There are those among them who appear to see nothing inconsistent in the demand that Great Britain alone should discard her nuclear weapons, while continuing to enjoy the protection of the nuclear deterrent in the hands of the United States. In support of this idea, the theory is adduced that such a noble gesture on our part would inspire others to follow our example. Anyone who can seriously believe that it would have the smallest effect on our potential enemies is surely somewhat naïve, to say the least. Nor is there any reason to suppose it would have any more effect on our friends.

Those who have any faith in moral "gestures" of this kind should study the historical examples, which have always proved useless. No one would take such a gesture at its face value, and we would not get the slightest credit for it. The Kremlin would be delighted and would not abate one whit the intensity of their development and production of nuclear weapons. Among our allies, we would be accused of lacking moral and physical courage, and our influence in the counsels of the Alliance would rapidly dwindle. Some would say that we were abandoning our obligations and making high-sounding excuses for turning away from an unpleasant job —*perfide Albion* again; others would say we were just saving money to improve living standards and to undercut them in foreign markets—the "nation of shopkeepers" as usual!

Moreover—and perhaps this is a more immediately practical point—it is our policy to get the disarmament negotiations started again; we hope to be sitting at the discussion table in the near future with the Russians, trying to persuade them to agree to an all-round reduction of armaments under a system of control and inspection. Is it really likely to lead to success in those negotiations if we begin by throwing away our strongest card now, by discarding our primary bargaining factor? One could hardly imagine the Russians responding: "Look, these splendid fellows have disarmed already.

Come on, we must play the game and follow their good example."

In my view, if there is one thing calculated to ensure the failure of any attempt to get the Communists to reduce their armaments, it is unilateral disarmament of any kind by any one of the Allies.

As for the moral issue, could it ever be morally defensible to use these appalling weapons? One cannot be dogmatic about this. But the real point here is the one I have already made—that the hydrogen bomb exists not to be used in war but to prevent war. I confess to being somewhat out of my depth on this moral issue, as, I suspect, are most of those who talk so glibly about it. I can only fall back on the views of a great religious leader and Christian, the late Archbishop Garbett of York, with whom I once discussed this subject. He made no secret of his utter abhorrence of nuclear war. Yet, in a debate in the House of Lords in 1955, he had this to say about it: "At the moment, the possession of the bomb seems to be the one possibility of preserving peace in the years immediately ahead. If so, it would be madness to close the door to this possibility."

Meanwhile, as a practical policy, we must never weaken—as we perhaps have tended to do in some stages of recent disarmament discussions—in our determination to retain adequate nuclear-deterrent capacity, not only until our opponents have reduced their conventional armaments to a true relative level with ours, but also for much longer, until political *rapprochement* has reached a point of understanding and permanence at which it is safe to assume that an appeal to force is no longer likely. This would mean for a very long time, but maybe not as long as it now appears; in any event, we must not allow our disappointment or impatience to blind us to the facts of life. A balance of military advantage throughout the process of disarmament is well and good—in fact, it is essential; but it must not be carried prematurely to an extreme that would put us at the disadvantage which I have suggested was a prime motive behind Khrushchev's comprehensive disarmament proposal of 1959.

In the area of nuclear disarmament, the Russian attitude —despite appearances to the contrary—has been quite consistent. Its one inconsistency was their rejection in 1947 of the Baruch plan, for which the reason may have been a compound of their innate suspiciousness and a belief that the plan was not permanently workable anyway (and they were probably right). Since then, their policy has varied to suit changing circumstances from time to time, but the object has always been that any measure of nuclear disarmament must involve military advantage for themselves. To that end, every single Russian proposal for dealing with the means of delivery has included, and still includes, the elimination of bases on foreign soil—primarily, of course, American bomber bases. They have now gone beyond the stage of relative nuclear inferiority, when their policy could be summarized by the words "ban the bomb," a theme that dominated Communist propaganda as well as their disarmament proposals. Since then, they have rung the changes on such points as the stage at which nuclear disarmament should be introduced into the program—a tactical move made when they saw an opportunity of exploiting differences of opinion on the subject among the Allies.

What I am really getting at is that the nuclear weapon should be the last to go; and if we insist on that point for ourselves, we must, of course, concede it to our opponents. Let me repeat, we must never run the risk of making war profitable again. This means that final nuclear disarmament cannot be safely accepted for a very long time to come. And meanwhile, we must retain an adequate measure—though we hope on a diminishing scale—of what has been usefully called "transitional deterrence" on either side.

Chapter 5

The Home Front

I NOW PROPOSE to explore a few lines of action that seem to me desirable to counter the Communist "peaceful" offensive in our own countries. Later, I shall go on to consider related problems on the continent of Europe and in the less-developed nations of the world.

To make a general point first: Our actions in the political, social, and economic spheres—whether at home or abroad—should not be inspired merely by anti-Communism. That kind of negative basis is a poor one for any policy. In point of fact, all the activities most likely to be effective in defeating Communism are those we should undertake purely on their own merits—things we ought to do even if Communism did not exist—and to give them an anti-Communist label often makes them more difficult to do. By no means can we always kill two birds with one stone, but in this case nearly always. The policies we adopt to achieve our own ends, to bring about the kind of world in which we want our children and grandchildren to live, are also those best calculated to defeat the aims of international Communism.

Domestic policy, even in Britain, is a subject on which I obviously cannot speak with real authority. It is the province of the statesman, and not of the soldier. But perhaps I may be permitted to express a few tentative views from the standpoint of the ordinary man, addressing myself mainly to the problems of Great Britain (though I suspect that the points on which I shall touch have parallels in most other countries of the Alliance).

First, the constructive minorities in our own lands should be more active in educating the masses to the realities of the Communist menace, particularly regarding the various spearheads of that attack which are proving all too successful in penetrating our own social systems. I am not one who sees a Communist under every bed. I do not call for witch-hunts (we have not yet measured the harm McCarthyism in the United States did to our common cause), or for such extremes as declaring the Communist Party illegal; both the Party members and their right-wing opposite numbers, such as the morons of the Mosley faction and the self-styled League of Empire Loyalists (which no doubt have their parallels in other lands), tend to defeat their own objects by their own inanities. What is urgently needed is primarily a public-relations job that, for the most part, can be better done by private organizations—including, of course, the press, radio, and television—rather than by governments, though the governments should be willing to support them, especially by supplying information, as long as it is not done in such a way as to make them suspect as covert government agencies.

An obvious example of the kind of activity that, in effect, aids Communism and is being very inadequately combatted is that of the unilateralists, neutralists, and nuclear disarmers. These are people with a mission—no less fervent for being misguided—and they work ceaselessly on their friends and acquaintances, on their fellow employees in offices, shops, and factories. By word of mouth, by cleverly drafted pamphlets, and by mass demonstrations, they reach the uninformed multitudes, who seldom read books like this or articles on defense and foreign policy in serious newspapers and periodicals. Those of us who do understand the danger and fallacies of this propaganda should match the energy of the unilateralists. And those who have most to lose by the triumph of neutralism should be prepared to support the too few organizations already at work in this field, and to finance speakers, pamphlets, advertisements in the popular press, and television features. It is a dangerous fallacy to assume that the present trend can safely be ignored, even in America. Complacency and apathy in this area, as in so many others, are powerful allies of Communism.

The range and significance of these pacifist and neutralist demonstrations should not be overestimated. They represent no more than a tiny fraction of British public opinion. Banner-wavers and pavement-squatters unfortunately have a news value in the press and on television that is out of all proportion to their real importance. It would be fantastic to imagine that Britain is in any danger of being unfaithful to the Alliance. But these movements have their dangers, for they are liable to spread if they are not intelligently countered. It is not inconceivable that war could result from miscalculation—from misjudgment by an aggressor of the resolution and moral fiber of our people. And in this respect, the nuclear disarmers are unwitting enemies of peace.

The members of these groups are probably unaware of the harm they are doing. Certainly, it is all to the good that some people of all ages—and particularly young people—have the enthusiasm, public spirit, and willingness to accept sacrifice for a cause that they consider beneficial to their community and to mankind in general. One of our troubles today is that there are not more people like this. Those we have should be encouraged—but encouraged to fight the real evils. There is no shortage, in either Britain or America, of good causes cry-ing out for champions, of dangerous evils that should be exposed and fought without playing into Communist hands: color prejudice and racial discrimination; the brutal excesses of "Teddy-boy" hooliganism; irresponsible and ignorant parents who contribute heavily to the growing problem of juvenile delinquency; the selfish "I'm-all-right-Jack" attitude that is concerned only with pillaging the common till while contributing the irreducible minimum to the common effort; the unofficial strikes that victimize decent workmen too timid or too loyal to resist them; the sex mania and cheap sensationalism that characterize much of the mass press; the senseless toll of death on the highways. There are plenty of such ogres and dragons waiting to be slain by the young knights in shining armor, their no less enthusiastic girl friends, and their clerical and academic captains, without their tilting at the windmills of nuclear strategy—about which they probably know just as much as I do about "rock and roll." It would, I'm afraid, be vain to suggest that, if they must sit on the pavement outside the Ministry of Defence, they should do so with the object of persuading the government to reintroduce conscription and take all the other very expensive steps necessary to raise the much larger conventional forces that alone might make some sense of nuclear disarmament.

But the essential, if their activities are to be redirected to serve useful and constructive ends, is that they should realize the true implications of what they are now doing. And to that end there is much that could be done by men and women of understanding and good will, if they were prepared to devote half as much energy to propagating the facts as the nuclear disarmers are to spreading their propaganda.

"There is nothing more easy to subvert than democratic processes." Addressing myself mainly, but not exclusively, to the conditions in Britain and realizing that I am venturing on thin ice, I must ask the following question: In view of the openly declared object of Communist policy, so aggressively reiterated in the Moscow declaration, can we afford to stand by indefinitely and allow Communist subversion to take advantage of the protection afforded by our democratic processes to destroy them? That is exactly what seems to be happening. I refer to the attack on our economy and standard of living by Communist-inspired disputes in industry. The trade unions have done, in the past century, and on the whole are still doing an indispensable and invaluable job; they are, in effect, a fourth estate of the British realm, and their leaders include men of real statesmanship and courage. They came into existence in order to protect and improve the standard of living of the working people—and how badly they were needed for that purpose! Are they today, at least in Britain, measuring up to what, in any common-sense view, should be the modern version of their function, to protect our national economy by helping to raise productivity and improve the standard of living of our people *as a whole* (without which that of their 8 million members is bound to decline)? How long can we stand by and watch Communist agents take advantage of the apathy, the lack of a sense of responsibility of the vast majority of trade unionists, to whittle away at the foundations of our industrial life?

Consider the endless dock strikes in America and Australia, as well as in Britain. Doesn't it make sense from the Communist point of view, in the attack on the democracies who depend so much for their strength and prosperity on sea communications, to bring activity to a standstill on the waterfronts of the Western world? Look at the senseless demarcation disputes in the shipyards that have done so much to bring down Great Britain from her former proud place as the greatest shipbuilding nation; the grip of Communism on the key Electrical Trades Union; the constant unofficial stoppages organized by Communist and fellow-traveling shop stewards in the motor and other key industries; the strike of tally clerks in the Port of London, which dealt such a body blow to British export trade, while Frank Cousins was away wrecking the Labour Party at Scarborough as a prelude to a brotherly trip to Moscow.

Can anyone claim that a system of trade unionism under which these things are almost everyday occurrences is in no need of modernization? Is it enough to take the line that this is a matter for the unions themselves to put right? Have they shown any signs of tackling the job during the past decade? How long must we give them to wake up to the reality of this threat to their own existence? Was this sort of thing envisaged when our industrial legislation was passed in earlier days? Was it for this that the Trades Disputes Act of 1906 freed trade unions from liability for damages arising out of actions by their agents in the course of a strike?

No doubt, I shall be told: "My dear fellow, any really experienced politician would tell you that to dabble in this sort of thing is political dynamite." I remain unimpressed by that argument. In the last fifty years, my generation has seen really experienced politicians leading us from muddle into monumental muddle, getting us involved in two world wars (of which at least the second was totally unnecessary if the politicians had had any guts). I am the last to despise politicians; I have been privileged to know statesmen, like Mr. Macmillan and Lord Attlee, with vision, courage, and—the first qualification for any position of great responsibility—the capacity to remain unrattled in the face of crisis. At the worst moment of our history, we were blessed with one politician who understood that the way to appeal to Englishmen in adversity is to tell them the truth. I believe that if our politicians and the Trade Union Congress told the people the truth about these unofficial strikes and other glaring anomalies of the trade-union system today and took a firm line with them, they would be astonished at the response they would get from the nation as a whole, including the great majority of union members.

The other dragon on the home front that I want to mention—and this has a direct and obvious bearing on our relations with the uncommitted half of the world—is the color bar. It is, I believe, no exaggeration to state that racial prejudice is Communism's best ally. If there is one issue more than any other that will be of transcendent importance in the struggle for peaceful coexistence in the coming years, it is the battle for the minds of the teeming millions in the newly emergent nations of Asia and Africa. The Communists are straining every nerve, not without some success, to defeat us in that battle. I will deal later with anticolonial sentiment as a Communist weapon to divide the West, and with certain aspects of policy vis-à-vis the uncommitted nations. My aim here is to suggest some things we must first do at home.

What I have to say on this subject is not based merely on altruism, nor does it stem from a guilt complex. This is a matter of sheer common sense and enlightened self-interest— the interest not only of winning the Cold War, but also of exploiting the tremendous opportunities for the trade by which we live that an increase in the standard of living among the enormous populations of the uncommitted countries would offer us. If Communism did not exist, if no question of decency or the Christian ethic were involved, it would still remain simple, hard-headed business sense to do everything possible to treat the colored peoples as friends and to help to establish on firm ground the economies of their new nations.

We would do well to recognize that the Western world suffers—no doubt for irrational reasons, but nevertheless unmistakably—from some handicaps in this struggle. Even without the lies and distorted half-truths of Communist propaganda, the endless cries of "colonial imperialism," there is to the peoples of the emergent nations some appeal in the idea of a vast country like Russia, not so long ago almost as undeveloped as their own, that has pulled itself up by its own bootstraps to the status of one of the world's two greatest military and industrial powers—and all this achieved under a Communist system of government. This appeal has been powerfully reinforced by the triumph of Communism in China. These simple people know nothing of the barbarities and injustices that lie behind the rise of Communist authority. They respect power; and if Russia and China are not loved, but are indeed feared, they are also respected. Moreover, however unreasonably and unjustly, the colonial background of some European NATO powers weighs in the balance against them. Nor is the United States by any means free from this taint (a statement that may astonish and affront some Americans, but one that can be substantiated), and "American imperialism" is now a major villain of the piece in modern Communist philosophy. Hardly anyone in Asia or Africa (except for those in the Soviet colonies in Central Asia) is aware of the truth that Russia is one of the most brutally oppressive colonial powers in history. The constant harping on the anticolonialist theme in Communist propaganda awakens an echo in the hearts of peoples whose attitude toward their former rulers is colored by what has been described as a "trauma of wounded pride."

That they were more badly governed, and often more cruelly oppressed, by their own rulers before the advent of the colonial power (and, in some cases, still are after its departure) may be true—for example, few things in any colonial rule could equal the treatment of "untouchables" in India—but it is irrelevant. The articulate and educated minorities (and they, whether we like it or not, are the people who count) prefer self-government to good government—and it is overcynical to ascribe this simply to the natural urge for "jobs for the boys." We may deplore, but we must accept, the rise of nationalism in Asia and Africa as one of the facts of life, and we have to come to terms with it as best we can.

The Communists are working busily and sparing no expense to win over these peoples by much more than just propaganda—by economic aid, theoretically free of strings; by grants and loans at low rates of interest, so easy for a nation with a wholly controlled economy; by the supply of specialists and technical advisers, always missionaries of the Communist religion; and by attracting young people from the new nations for training in Soviet and satellite schools and colleges, where Communist indoctrination is as much a part of the curriculum as technical or professional education.

There is no reason for us to be alarmed about this, for we are not doing so badly along these lines ourselves. Britain has brought to nationhood within the Commonwealth more people than Russia has brought under her colonial rule in the past twenty years. Economic aid from Western countries, including a huge volume of private capital investment, has been far more generous than Russian aid and—despite some brashness, crudities, and blunders—more genuinely free from strings. We have supplied far more advisers and helpers for the economies of emergent countries; and the numbers of young people from these nations—students and undergraduates, trainees in law, medicine, and industry—now studying in Western countries enormously outnumber those in Russia (there are well over 20,000 of them in Britain alone). We have one great asset in the Commonwealth, and another in the English and French languages, which fortunately are infinitely more widely known and used in Asia and Africa than is Russian. One need only note how many of the leading personalities of the emergent nations have a background of education at Oxford and Cambridge or the Inns of Court, at the Sorbonne, or at American universities.

But we must avoid complacency. We must understand what we are up against and be prepared to accept some sacrifice and personal inconvenience to deal with it. Perhaps most difficult, we must adjust our minds and habits of thought to present-day realities if we are going to win this battle. We must realize that it is in our own interest, as well as being our duty as responsible citizens of the world, to build up the economies of these underdeveloped countries, rather than to make them more dependent on ours; to equip them for effective self-government by helping them to develop the viable economy without which national independence is an empty façade; and to modernize and amplify their own ways of life, without trying to impose on them the British or American or French way of life.* Above all, we must free ourselves from color prejudice before it costs us the loss—as it alone perhaps could—of the tremendous advantage we still enjoy.

The vital and intricate problem of assistance in an economic buildup of the underdeveloped countries is beyond the scope of this book. A great deal has been and is being done by Western nations—notably, the United States, Britain, and France—and we may draw encouragement from the evident determination of the new U.S. Administration to continue and improve upon the initiatives of previous ones along these lines. I will only touch on certain aspects of this task as it affects our home fronts in the struggle of peaceful coexistence.

The core of the problem is that we delude ourselves if we imagine we can continue to enjoy, still less improve upon, our present standard of living while half the world's population has a standard of living not far removed from that of the

---

* One wonders whether America's attitude in this respect may not be slightly distorted by her experience in Japan, which is so different from other Asian countries.

Stone Age. This does not mean that the welfare state must go, or that the emergent countries can look to us to solve their problems without doing anything for themselves. Asoka Mehta, an Indian representative at the last unofficial Commonwealth Relations Conference in New Zealand in 1959, made it clear that these countries well understand that they must pull themselves up by their own bootstraps. Our job is to help them get airborne; once they are off the ground, they will gather speed and eventually fly by themselves. But we cannot do this through deficit financing; unless we sustain and improve our own economies and keep our balance of payments on a sound footing, we shall be unable to help these peoples, however much we may want to. What we surely can and must do is to accept some reduction in the *rate of increase* of our own standards of living in the interest of those in poorer countries—which, in the long run, will be in our own interest.

But there is more involved in the development of the emergent countries than just grants, loans, and private investment. Perhaps a more urgent need in these countries is for the development of technical and professional skills of their own. They need our experienced pilots to help them get airborne; but if they are to fly by themselves, they must have crews of their own. Particularly in the African countries, the desperate need is not only for university graduates and professional men and women (many of whom are already being trained in the West, though we must take many more), but for technicians, skilled artisans, and the various lower grades of administrative personnel. "In Tanganyika," said Julius Nyerere recently, "it is not my kingdom for a horse, it is my administration for twenty stenographers." Again, in an aviation metaphor, it is not only pilots and navigators that they need, but engineers and servicing personnel.

This is a gap we can certainly help to fill at reasonable cost and not much inconvenience to ourselves. A movement is now being initiated in Britain—and we hope it will extend to other countries of the Commonwealth, as well as to the United States—to meet this need. The idea is that throughout our country, great industrial concerns, small manufacturers, farms, banks, insurance companies, hospitals, public services, and government departments—in effect, every variety of occupation that makes up the efficient working of the modern state—would take on one or two Africans and teach them the basis of the techniques involved.

There are three essential conditions in this scheme. First, Africans taking advantage of it will not be allowed to exercise their right as Commonwealth citizens to remain in Britain; the whole point of bringing them here will be that they should return and put their training at the service of their own countries. Secondly, married men are to bring their wives, who will be given useful experience in hospitals, child-welfare centers, teachers' colleges, etc. And finally, as far as possible, the visitors are to be lodged in British homes and assimilated into the life of the community, for the success of the project will ultimately be determined at the level of personal relations.

Such a plan clearly involves many difficulties, and it is still too early to say whether it will prove practicable or acceptable to the British people. The hope is that a pilot scheme may shortly be launched on a modest scale, from which much should be learned. But here is an imaginative idea that, if it can be brought to fruition, could do wonders to consolidate the Commonwealth ideal and defeat the dark designs of Communism in Africa.

However, these young people—like the thousands now in the universities and technical colleges, apprentice schemes, medical and law schools of Britain—will return to their countries either as ambassadors of good will toward the West or as embittered victims of inferiority complexes, providing rich soil for the seeds of Communism; their attitudes will be determined by the treatment they receive while they are here. Let us frankly admit that all too often they are treated badly here (and, no doubt, in the United States)—sometimes thoughtlessly, but too often deliberately because of their color. "One of the less spurious appeals that Soviet Communism has for politically immature peoples is the theoretical and to a large extent genuine absence of the color bar from Soviet practice."* It would be dishonest to pretend that there is no color prejudice in Britain. Nor is it any good pretending that this is an easy problem. *But it must be solved.*

Its solution calls for a program of popular indoctrination on a nationwide scale—by governments and churches, employer groups and trade unions, colleges and schools, and every medium of public information. Color prejudice and racial discrimination must be stamped out, or we shall lose this desperately critical battle for the minds of men. It is just as simple as that.

Finally, this is only one side of the problem—the other being our attitude toward our own colored citizens. It is not for me to tell Americans what they ought to do. But I hope they are under no delusions. Every anti-Negro riot in Little Rock or New Orleans puts a God-sent weapon into the hands of Communism in Africa—and in Latin America and the Caribbean as well. I have been told by American friends that I should look at these things differently if I lived in a Southern state with a Negro majority. Very likely. But let them remember that British inhabitants of parts of Africa are up against that situation to an even greater degree.

We in Britain are not blameless. We have our Notting Hills. And it is easier for us to talk because our problem is not as great as America's. Our troubles may grow—but never to such dimensions. Let us in England never be tempted to yield to the demand to cut off colored immigration from the Commonwealth. The right of every Commonwealth citizen—whatever his color, race, or creed—to free entry and equal

---

* *Strategy for the West*, p. 55.

access to any occupation or profession in the United Kingdom is an essential part of the Commonwealth ideal. There may be a case for imposing certain restrictions, such as those existing in every other Commonwealth country, on grounds of criminal record or disease or the inability of the immigrant to support himself. But once we impose any restrictions on grounds of color or race, it will be a boon to Communism and the beginning of the end of the Commonwealth.

Chapter 6

First Steps in Europe

WHILE THE ULTIMATE issue of peaceful coexistence may well be decided in Asia, Africa, and Latin America, Europe retains its cardinal importance as the area where the two great political and military power blocs are in actual contact. It may contain the key that can unlock the first gate in the rampart of hostility and suspicion dividing East from West. But it is also in itself a vital—basically the most vital—front in the Cold War.

In considering Western strategy for Europe, let us recall the object defined earlier, noting that its achievement involves two avenues of approach, each equal in importance: disarmament, or arms control; and resolution of the political (or geopolitical) differences between the NATO powers and the Soviet Union. The former is the means, the latter the end. But in my view, these two, the end and the means, happen to be complementary, each a part of the same process in which measures to achieve either contribute to the achievement of both.

It would be an oversimplification to claim that the end as so defined is primarily a question of restoration of national sovereignties throughout Europe; indeed, an overemphasis on sovereignty is one of the curses of the modern world and, as Lord Hailsham has pointed out, is often distorted to serve the purposes of international Communism. Nevertheless, it can hardly be denied (except, perhaps, by the extreme advocates of a "united states" of Europe, which does not seem likely within the foreseeable future) that political composition in Europe must involve national independence as well as political, social, and economic interdependence among the European nations—that is, independence for smaller states from foreign military domination and illegitimate external pressure by more powerful ones. Meanwhile, military interdependence remains an indispensable foundation for any building of economic or political cooperation.

This is not the place to discuss such questions as the relations between EEC and EFTA or the degree of political cooperation that should accompany economic integration (federation or De Gaulle's "imposing confederation"). It should suffice here to make the obvious point that a vital essential is that economic groupings should not be allowed to destroy the unity of Europe or weaken the bonds of the Atlantic Alliance in the face of the Communist threat. We would be well advised to remember the virtues of gradualness, for we have seen before in this European context at least one example—the fate of the European Defense Community—of how overenthusiasm for premature solutions and overemphasis on supranational institutions can bring noble purposes to nothing.

Military interdependence within NATO, however, has not recently kept pace with measures of economic interdependence within the Six and the Seven—has, indeed, of late been honored more in the breach than in the observance. This is not to say it has not been honored at all: We see it manifested in the integration at command and staff levels, in the infrastructure program, and to some extent in the weapons field. But there are still serious gaps. And my aim here is to suggest how further military interdependence might be combined with, and contribute to, modest first steps in the direction of political *détente* and arms control—or, to be more accurate, in the first instance arms stabilization. I would suggest that here is a field in which we can exploit, to the advantage of both sides, most of the areas of interest common to ourselves and the U.S.S.R.—particularly the fear of surprise attack, the "Nth-power" problem, and disarmament—and, moreover, one in which we might be able to make a start without wasting time on negotiation to secure Russian agreement.

The final communiqué issued by the NATO Ministers of Foreign Affairs, Defense, and Finance after their meeting in December, 1960, stated: "The North Atlantic nations must be able to respond to any attack with whatever force might be appropriate. There must be a proper balance in the forces of the Alliance of nuclear and conventional strength to provide the required flexibility." Further, the Atlantic Council noted with great interest the U.S. suggestion for "an MRBM multilateral force [including a number of Polaris submarines under NATO control] for consideration by the Alliance" and "instructed the Permanent Representatives to study the suggestion *and related matters* [italics added] in detail."

It is, I think, clear from the wording of the British White Paper on defense* that the reference to "related matters" constituted, in effect, an instruction to the permanent staffs —the political representatives, the Standing Group, and the Military Committee in Permanent Session—to review not only the American suggestion but also the general strategy that should determine the organization and equipment of the Allied forces in Europe. The results of that review will pre-

* *Report on Defence* (Cmnd. 1288, 1961).

sumably be made known at the next Atlantic Council meeting in Oslo in May, 1961 (before publication of this book).* But I would like to suggest certain criteria by which they should be judged and (in the next chapter) to submit some recommendations about the strategic pattern to which I personally hope they will lead. Let us bear in mind throughout that in order to accord fully with every aspect of NATO policy, the decisions of the Council should contribute not only to the clarification of strategic policy and improvements in the organization and equipment of General Norstad's forces, but also to progress in the direction of arms control.

First, we must hope that any advance will be determined by the strategy of limited objectives. I will not belabor that point further, except to repeat that our first aim should be a modest beginning toward removal of the barrier of mistrust between the two power blocs, if that can be begun—as I believe it can—at a risk no more (and probably less) serious than that inherent in the indefinite acceptance of the status quo, and without extending concessions of any kind that are not matched on the Soviet side.

Secondly, while fear, under present conditions (which we must strive to ameliorate), is a stabilizing factor up to a point —that, after all, is what deterrence means—if our military policy is such as to aggravate the fear beyond that certain point, it might defeat its own object and conceivably lead to the very thing it is designed to deter. There is no doubt that a genuine cause of fear—and one that probably contributes as much as anything to the aggravation of tensions in the military area—is the conception of surprise attack. No one can deny that this fear is a real one on the Western side—perhaps less in the case of the phlegmatic and rather

---

* No definite conclusions on this subject were reached in time for the May meeting, and it is still being examined by the staffs.

unimaginative British than (quite naturally) among our European allies, particularly Germany, and (less naturally) in the United States. It is less easy to understand that it is a genuine fear on the Soviet side.

Perhaps we should define here what we mean by "surprise attack." I have never been able to take seriously the possibility of what is sometimes called the "bolt from the blue"—the idea that we might awake one morning to find that in one fell swoop all our retaliatory forces—bombers, missiles, Polaris submarines, and aircraft carriers all over the world—and most of our population had been wiped out. This utterly unrealistic conception seems to be at the bottom of much misunderstanding regarding the credibility of our deterrent policy. No one can say with any certainty that the men in the Kremlin would not undertake such action if they could be absolutely sure of carrying it out successfully. But I doubt that they would. Apart from any ethical considerations, which perhaps might not deter them, they would have to reckon with the effects on Russia of the tremendous radioactive fallout. They certainly do not possess the weapons for such an attack now, and moreover, even when they do have the capability, they still could not be sufficiently sure of the total success necessary. There are pitfalls in the kind of slide-rule strategy that assesses the number of Soviet bombers and missiles against the number of Allied bases, etc., and arrives at the positive conclusion that the former could eliminate the latter. Things simply do not work out that way in war. And the consequences to the Russians of even partial failure would be so catastrophic that I do not believe they would ever make the attempt. In any event, this is like speculating about a possible "act of God"—there is no practicable insurance against it, and we can only live with it as we do with the possibility of another planet's colliding with our own.

We know that there is no prospect of the West's launching a surprise attack. Despite occasional rash and irresponsible talk in the past, "the American people," as Bernard Brodie has pointed out,* "have obviously made a decision, with little overt debate but with quite remarkable unanimity, against any form of preventive war." In my opinion, the only surprise attack for which there is any possibility is a "preemptive" attack by the Russians; and I consider the recent rather woolly trend of NATO strategic thinking, particularly in relation to the so-called "tactical atomic weapons" (TAW), partly responsible for this possibility. It is not inconceivable that in a period of critical tension, when war appeared to be imminent—if, for instance, the Kremlin leaders had gotten themselves into a position from which it seemed impossible to back down—the Russians might conclude that, since NATO was going to use nuclear weapons anyway (and in certain circumstances intended to use them first), they should be quicker on the draw, strike first, and risk the consequences.

I do not consider this remotely probable. It assumes, to begin with, that the Soviet Union will create a situation in which total war is inevitable—which I do not believe it has any intention of doing. Moreover, this would not really constitute a surprise attack. It is surely unrealistic to assume that, under the conditions envisaged, the Allies would take no precautions; our bombers would be alerted and dispersed, the submarines and carriers at sea and the missile crews ready for the countdown—in short, we would probably reduce the vulnerability of our retaliatory forces by a factor of more than half.

Nevertheless, though highly improbable, such an attack is not inconceivable. People do very stupid things when they are frightened, and the Russians have some reason to fear the military prowess of Germany, particularly if it is reinforced by tactical nuclear arms. One cannot be absolutely

---

* *Strategy in the Missile Age* (Princeton, N.J.: Princeton University Press, 1959; London: Oxford University Press, 1959).

sure that, having gotten themselves into a corner, fear might not urge them to the action they would never contemplate in other circumstances. If this is even a remote possibility, we should do something about it. It is in this context that I will suggest later on a measure of arms control by which, without increased risk to our own security, we could do something to erode this sector of the wall of fear and mistrust, bringing our military policy more in line with our political object of reducing tension and reaching a settlement in Europe.

The *Concise Oxford Dictionary* defines the word "tactics" as "the art of disposing military or naval forces in actual contact with the enemy." On the basis of this or any other intelligent definition, the description of fighter-bombers or missiles with ranges of 1,500 miles or more as "tactical" takes considerable liberty with the English language.

It is pointless now to deplore Western initiative in introducing these TAW; the development was probably inevitable sooner or later. I would like to see them abolished if and when that becomes at all possible, and I think this should remain an intermediate objective of our arms-control policy. But we must face the fact that matters have now gone so far —including the equipment of the Red Army with TAW in substitution for conventional units—that abolition in the near future is simply not a practicable objective. It is certainly only realistic however, with the rise of weapons like Honest John and Davy Crockett, to recognize the consequent loss of real meaning in the old differentiation between conventional and nuclear weapons. We must find some new way of categorizing these weapons (and tactical and strategic weapons as well) that will not only be conducive to clarity, but will also help us to limit and control the weapons, as a first step toward ultimate abolition. This is not merely a question of giving a rose another name. It is, I believe, a practical move toward

eliminating the confusion and misunderstanding that now be-
devils NATO strategy.

To elaborate this point, I must delve a bit into recent history. The application of the word "tactical" to the air forces
of World War II put some strain on its precise definition.
But the categorization of air forces as tactical and strategic
was useful in resolving what now appears to have been a
somewhat unnecessary squabble between those (particularly
in the army) whose duty it was to concern themselves
with the needs of the battle and the Air Staff, whose interest (sometimes perhaps unduly single-minded) in building
up the bomber offensive against the heart of Germany was
certainly not uninfluenced by their awareness that it was
primarily by this means that we could achieve the degree of
air superiority essential to success on the battlefield. What
followed has a direct bearing, I think, on the present-day
problems of NATO. The air forces were divided into "tactical" and "strategic" forces (both words being adopted for
lack of better ones). The sole function of the former, mainly
light bombers and fighter bombers, was to cooperate with
and support the armies engaged in land campaigns. The latter,
mainly medium and heavy bombers, were assigned to the
direct assault on the enemy country—related to but not closely
connected with the battle—as they are today. But it was inherent in the flexibility of air forces (which, alas, has diminished in recent years) that the division was not absolute.
The supreme commanders in the various theaters of war had
a call upon those components of the strategic air forces based
in or near their areas, but normally engaged in the air offensive against Germany, to supplement the efforts of the tactical
air forces where the task involved was beyond the latter's
capacity. There were many instances when such call was
made—both in defense (for example, against the Ardennes
offensive of 1944) or in attack (before Overlord); indeed,
before the Normandy landings, a high proportion of the effort

of the strategic air forces was diverted to support of the
invasion by paralyzing the enemy's communications behind
the lodgment area.

In my opinion, this experience has been inadequately applied to today's conditions. There has always been some
question as to whether the present strategic air forces would
be available for support in battle—and if so, when, how, and
to what extent. In 1950, as Chief of the Air Staff, I gave an
assurance to a conference of NATO generals that the first
task of Bomber Command would be collaboration with the
NATO armies and air forces in stemming a Russian invasion
of Western Europe.* My impression is that SACEUR now
has no such assurance. I may be wrong, but Bomber Command is certainly an integral component in the Allied retaliatory striking force. General Norstad does have his own
tactical air forces, including even a few Valiant medium
bombers of the RAF, and they may be considered adequate
to any task that might be imposed upon them, but this seems
unlikely to me. If they were, there would be no reason for the
present discussions about medium-range missiles or Polaris
submarines in his command. The Russians have much stronger
tactical air forces, including transonic medium-range bombers; their armies have recently been reorganized to include
many nuclear missiles with ranges of 400 miles and more; and
they must at least be assumed to be planning to locate missiles
with much longer ranges in their Western defense zones. It
may be that General Norstad has some secret assurance of cooperation by Strategic Air Command or Bomber Command.
In any case, I find it difficult to believe that if SACEUR's
forces were engaged in desperate battle with greatly superior
enemy forces surging across Germany, the whole of the
strategic air forces would really be able to concentrate on a
counterattack against the heart of Russia, as though there

---

* See Slessor, *The Great Deterrent* (London: Cassell & Co., 1957; New
York: Frederick A. Praeger, 1957), pp. 108–9.

were no ground action in Western Europe. Here again, there is a lesson to be learned from the experience of Bomber Command during the invasion of France in 1940.*

Though I will enlarge upon this subject later, the point I want to make now is that we should recategorize our forces as "strategic" and "battle" forces. "Strategic" is perhaps not the most suitable term, but it does convey the connotation, now widely familiar, of those forces whose task is the retaliatory counteroffensive against enemy territory. Battle forces would be those whose task is to participate in the land-air battle for the direct defense of Western Europe. And these should include a subcategory determined by range and yield —the real tactical weapons for use in actual contact with the enemy, and I would so classify the 8-inch howitzer and the truly tactical battlefield missiles like Corporal, Honest John, and Davy Crockett, and all other weapons nuclear or otherwise of lesser range and yield. It is in this sense that I will use the term "tactical forces" from now on, differentiating where necessary between the nuclear and the nonnuclear ones. An important point about these "battlefield" weapons is that I think they could be used, even in limited operations in Europe, without the *certainty* (though, of course, not without the *possibility*) of unlimited escalation, which I do not believe is true of other so-called "tactical weapons" of greater range and yield. In fact, because of them, the differentiation between defensive and offensive weapons may begin to make some sense for the first time in history.†

All this may seem unduly pedantic and professional; but I think such a recategorization of forces not only accords with common-sense realities, but should also serve to eliminate

---

* See Slessor, *The Central Blue* (London: Cassell & Co., 1956; New York: Frederick A. Praeger, 1957), pp. 294–96.

† It seems to be too much to hope that in the foreseeable future anyone will have the sense to replace the present ridiculous lethal and destructive weapons with the nonlethal, incapacitating chemicals that already exist.

much of the confusion and misunderstanding that now surrounds the subject.

Before going on to consider a NATO plan for Europe, let us determine what its limited object should be. While gratefully admitting NATO's accomplishments—without the Alliance, we might not still be free people—I make no secret of my belief that in the political field our policy in the past decade has been characterized by what M. Van Zeeland of Belgium described, at the Atlantic Congress of 1959, as "disappointing, obstinate, and even dangerous immobilism." It is not enough to prevent ourselves from being killed. We must reassume the initiative, which we have repeatedly surrendered to the enemy, remaining content merely to protect ourselves. There is a sword as well as a shield in political strategy, just as there is in military strategy—and no one ever won a fight by using a shield alone.

What I want to see happen in Europe (and on this point, at least, Field Marshal Montgomery and I agree) is for the Red Army to move back behind its own frontiers. For the moment, we need not worry about what are or should be the exact limits of those frontiers, but may as well accept the existing ones. We may feel pity for the peoples of the Baltic states for instance, the people of Vilna and Lvov in what was Eastern Poland, and the people of Bessarabia; but these are problems that must wait for a later stage of the journey. It may seem callous to describe them as details, but in the broad context of world settlement, that is what they are—however important they may be to the unfortunate inhabitants of those territories. To argue about them now would be completely fruitless: If we reach our final goal, these problems will settle themselves; if we allow them to prevent us from making a start, they will never be solved.

We must recognize that the final removal of the wall of

mistrust and hostility is going to take a very long time. Our intermediate aim should be to create a *cordon sanitaire*, a physical and political no-man's-land of militarily nonaligned independent buffer-states (what I have described in a previous book as "a sort of extension of Sweden southwards to the Black Sea"),* comprising Poland, Czechoslovakia, Hungary, Rumania, Bulgaria, and perhaps eventually a reunified Germany. But that is far too ambitious as a short-term objective. We should proclaim it as our aim and work to attain it as soon as possible. Meanwhile, our limited political object for now should be *to get the Red Army out of East Germany*. If that were achieved reasonably soon, we might well find that the liberation of the satellite states from Soviet military domination would come much sooner than now seems probable.

Germany is, indeed, at the heart of the European deadlock. I deplore the wrongs done to Germany through partition, and the Russian action in maintaining the division is, of course, inexcusable. But this is part of the price Germany must pay for Adolf Hitler, and I can feel no passionate indignation about it as such—any more, I suspect, than do many West Germans.

On the other hand, the divided nation remains a source of dangerous instability on the European scene, and for that reason we should do everything possible to reunify Germany as soon as possible. Moreover, the situation holds within it the delayed-action bomb of Berlin. I do not for a moment believe that the Russians would risk total war over Berlin. But it suits them admirably to make us believe they would— a classic example of how they play on our apparent inability to realize that total war is not any more a part of their design than it is of ours. Here is a point where they have the initiative, where they can blow hot and cold and exploit the delu-

---

* *Strategy for the West.*

sion of too many people in the West that we have no means of countering Russian pressure on Berlin short of total war; they can use it as a lever and bargaining factor if we are foolish enough to allow them to do so.

There is also the problem of the eastern frontier. Here again, the Germans should realize that few among their Western allies lose any sleep over their loss of the territories beyond the Oder-Neisse line. Our general attitude, I think, would be that the German people should have thought of this before they allowed their *Führer* to make his infamous deal with Stalin for the partition of Poland in 1939. Certainly, no Western government would dream of going to war on Germany's side over these territories—indeed, we would be among Germany's enemies if she ever attempted to regain them by force, which I know (and fully accept) that Dr. Adenauer's Government has repeatedly said it has no intention of doing.

Someday, perhaps, there may be a general peace settlement in which this matter will be adjusted. But I doubt that the territories will (or should) ever be returned to Germany. Meanwhile, though I realize that no West German politician of any party can say so openly—and, indeed, to do so might be regarded as surrendering a small though actually very unreal bargaining factor—the sooner the Germans content themselves with their position as a free and coequal partner in a great alliance of free nations, forgetting about their "lost territories," the healthier it will be for them and for the Alliance as a whole. It would surely be in Germany's own true interest if more of her allies followed in this respect the courageous lead of General de Gaulle.

If and when we do succeed in getting the Red Army out of East Germany, all sorts of problems will arise: relations between the present Federal Republic and the so-called German Democratic Republic, methods of bringing about ultimate reunification (for which there are some precedents in German history), control of Berlin, and measures to safeguard against the dangerous possibilities of internecine strife between East and West Germans. It would not necessarily be essential at once to impose upon East Germany a democratic system of internal government. And it would be too much to expect it to break off economic relations with the Soviet bloc. The beginnings of a solution may lie in an initial loose association dealing with such matters as transportation, communications, etc.

If I do not elaborate this subject further, it is not because I underrate the difficulties—obviously immense—but because I do not believe they are insuperable. In any event, if we adopt the solution suggested as our aim, there will be plenty of time for all the problems and difficulties to be considered and plans made in advance to surmount them by the appropriate authorities in NATO—and particularly in the German Federal Republic.

Chapter 7

A New Plan for NATO

LET US NOW CONSIDER a practical plan for NATO in Europe. I have suggested a limited political object that such a plan should be designed to achieve: to get the Red Army out of East Germany and to make a start in arms control. This can only be done through a gradual process. Meanwhile, we must guard against a sudden death blow being dealt to the process by Soviet military aggression or the threat of it. Thus, as an intermediate stage, NATO must be so consolidated and re-organized as to ensure the protection "of our allies and our friends against the whole spectrum of possible aggression and military threats, from the small local action which might be the beginning of larger and more dangerous adventures through 'nuclear blackmail' to nuclear war."*

We must first be clear about the military object that the NATO forces are—or should be—designed to serve. In particular, there should be no ambiguity about what the forces in Germany are there *for*. The definition of purpose quoted above, though perfectly sound, is too general; nor is it

* *Report on Defence.*

enough to say, though it is certainly true, that these forces are an essential part of the deterrent. What we—and more important, they—must know is the action they would be required to take in the event of aggression in any form. My point here is that no one, from the Supreme Commander downward, appears to be really clear about that vitally important question—and that the old and perfectly valid conception of the "sword and shield" in NATO seems to me in recent years to have gone dangerously adrift in interpretation.

Before attempting to justify this somewhat sweeping statement, I should define briefly the form I think aggression in Europe is likely to take. In doing so, we can simplify the problem if we confine our attention to the key front, the partition line in Central Europe. Although this is not the only front where aggression may occur, the principles governing our strategy there are equally applicable to the other fronts within the area of SHAPE responsibility.

If aggression were initially to take the form of massive assault, whether by nuclear air power or full-scale invasion of West Germany across the partition line, then there would be no problem; our action could only be to react against it immediately with every weapon in our armory. But it should be obvious by now that I do not see the remotest prospect of any such assault. General Norstad clearly shares the view that, if aggression occurs, it will take the initial form of what he has called "an incident, a clash, whether intentional or unintentional"—a minor infiltration to test our reactions, to see whether we in NATO have the unity and resolution to deal with it at once. It might, for instance, be a staged riot by "oppressed patriots" in some city near the partition line, supported by "peace-loving volunteers" from East Germany. If successful at first, it would be nourished and supported by Russia, and could then assume really dangerous proportions, perhaps amounting almost to limited local war. This sequence of events might even reach a point where the Kremlin conceivably (though I do not consider it probable) will have gotten itself into a position from which it may feel it cannot withdraw—and then the war would be on. However, if dealt with promptly and thoroughly, such an incident might well be disowned by the Kremlin as none of its affair—though we would surely be treated to the usual hectoring display over Radio Moscow and in the United Nations.

In order to understand the development of NATO strategy to meet this kind of aggression, it is again necessary to examine recent history. In the early 1950's, NATO policy in Europe was based on a conventional forward strategy involving the unrealistically high force-levels of the "Lisbon goals." At the same time, the Americans (in Strategic Air Command) and, to a lesser extent, the British (in Bomber Command) were building up atomic air striking power almost totally independent of NATO policy. However, the conclusion soon became inescapable that it made neither political nor economic sense to try to superimpose the new atomic strategy on the old conventional one. The revised conception—which became the "new look" in American and NATO strategic thinking and led ultimately to the military policy that still governs NATO strategy in Europe—originated in Whitehall. It is now no secret that the policy was to give priority to atomic air power and thus build up the strength necessary in that sphere to constitute a decisive deterrent to aggression, which at the same time would enable us to resist and counter aggression if the deterrent failed to deter. Clearly, as part of the deterrent, there had to be conventional forces in Germany, much smaller than the impracticable Lisbon goals, but substantially larger than the quite inadequate forces then available. The role of these forces was to prevent us from being confronted with the usual Communist *faits accomplis*—and, if the deterrent failed, to delay a Russian advance, thus allowing time for the strategic counteroffensive to take effect. Here was the original conception of the sword and the shield; and the crucial point to note is that no one ever envisaged that the conventional forces in Germany (the shield) would defend Europe against major aggression without the intervention of the strategic air forces (the sword).

The outlines of this relatively simple concept were subsequently somewhat blurred by three factors: the rise of Russian long-range air power to a level equal with that of the West; the development of TAW, accompanied by the fallacious theory that they lent overwhelming advantage to the defensive; and the lack of clarity (already mentioned) regarding whether or to what extent the strategic air forces would be diverted to objectives directly related to the defense of European territory. But the main strategic concept remains valid; and the idea of forcing the pause, in order to impose upon the aggressor the choice between the alternatives of negotiation or a conscious decision for total war, was a logical development of the delaying role of the shield.

The fact is, however, that after ten years of existence, NATO has the shield of the armies and tactical air forces in Europe, but it actually has no sword of its own. And it is this that is now causing much confused thought subjecting the Alliance to some strain. *Members* of NATO (America and Britain) have strategic air forces under their own control, and we do not doubt that these would be used against an aggressor in the NATO area. But our allies are not so sure of this; in fact, it is partly for this reason that the French are trying to build up a sword of their own, and there is a possibility that others may follow their lead.

While the Russians have a powerful strategic air force as well as the other tactical air and missile forces already mentioned, NATO itself has—apart from its relatively few tactical air forces and nuclear armed units on the ground—no equivalent forces under the control and direction of the Atlantic Council; and there can be no combined planning or formulation of policy within the Standing Group or Military Committee for the use of the sword in the defense of Europe. It is understandable, therefore, that General Norstad should want to do some planning for the use of a sword of his own. He can hardly be blamed for liking the idea that his forces in Europe should be equipped with weapons like Mace and Polaris, in addition to his bombers and fighter bombers, which already have similar ranges with nuclear loads.

The American suggestion of an MRBM force under the control of NATO, now under consideration, may (and I hope will) result in the provision to the Alliance of a sword under its own control. (I shall return to this point later.) Meanwhile, however, a vital essential is to decide what should be the proper function of the shield forces. The policy of sword and shield remains in the background; but it is perhaps only natural that a failure to complete the organization required to fulfill agreed NATO policy should be reflected in a lack of clarity in the development of that policy. I am inclined to think that the fault lies partly in these symbolic terms, which are always liable to different interpretations. There is a shield force, under the command of SACEUR; there is a sword force, not under NATO control. But while both are essential parts of the deterrent, they exist for almost entirely separate purposes. SACEUR's job in Europe is to be ready to fight a battle; and you cannot fight a battle with a shield alone, any more than a boxer can win a bout using only his defensive hand.

My own feeling is that the sooner we drop these terms (and confine sword and shield to the SHAPE insignia), the better. I have already suggested that the true strategic concept would be clearer if we used the term, "strategic force" (for want of a better one) to describe the retaliatory striking force for action against Russian territory and "battle force" to identify those forces whose duty in war would be the direct defense of Europe against invasion. The battle force itself would, of course, have a shield function, that of a covering and delaying force, as well as a sword function, that of counterattack (the soul of defense). But these are perfectly normal traditional characteristics of any military force. We might find also, as we did so often in World War II, that elements of the strategic force would have to be pulled in to support the battle force and prevent the war from being lost in Europe while it was being won in the heart of Russia. But the circumstances would be so different and the tempo of events so fast-moving that it would be unwise to count on such a contingency; and if, as seems evident, SACEUR's counterattack force is inadequate, then we have no alternative other than to increase it.

But there is more to this problem, and it is such an important one that it should be examined further. A reappraisal by SHAPE in 1957 of the forces required in Europe defined the functions of these forces in terms similar to those outlined above: deterrence, by keeping visible forces along the frontier; identification, by holding an incursion until it could be identified as serious; and retaliation, under which it was accepted that "the West would have no option but to use the strategic nuclear deterrent" (as *The Times* [London] put it).*

Within two years, however, General Norstad's conception of his responsibilities—or perhaps his directive from the Standing Group—appeared to have undergone a disconcerting change. In an important speech to the Atlantic Congress in London in June, 1959—repeated in similar though not identical terms to the NATO Parliamentarians in Paris on November 21, 1960—he defined these responsibilities in a way

---

* See also *The New York Times,* November 13, 1957, quoting General Norstad's speech in Cincinnati.

impossible to reconcile with the original concept or with the meaning of the reappraisal in 1957.

Outlining what he called "the basic objectives of any valid strategy in Europe," the Supreme Commander said: "First, in the event of an incident, a clash, whether intentional or unintentional, we must be able to force a pause, to compel a break in the continuity of the action that has started. . . . [The aggressor] must be compelled to realize that by continuing his action he chooses war with all its consequences to him. . . . The shield forces of NATO are designed to achieve these objectives." This, of course, is unexceptionable, and fully in accord with the original concept.

Later in his speech, General Norstad said: "The shield must be strong enough, and its resources sufficiently versatile, beyond all possible doubt, to deal *decisively* [italics added] with any attack short of the unmistakable, deliberate, all-out aggression which would invoke the heavy side of the deterrent [the retaliatory nuclear striking forces]." This seems to me much more open to question; we have here an ill-defined twilight phase between the pause and war. "Decisively"? "Any attack"? It could perhaps be argued that it depends on what is meant by "deliberate, all-out aggression"; but it unmistakably goes a great deal further than enforcing an interval for deliberation, holding out the option of negotiation or war.

However, when General Norstad says that one of the military functions of the shield (not of NATO, but of the *shield*) is to "defend the easternmost peoples and territories of the Alliance," which "involves holding Europe *against a full range of possible attack, up to aggression in its heaviest form* [italics added]," and that it must be "capable of dealing with both nuclear and nonnuclear situations," this is an entirely different matter and cannot possibly be reconciled with the original basic objective of the shield forces. These words can only mean that we have failed to enforce the pause and the enemy has, in fact, already chosen "war with all its consequences to him." It is explicit in the Supreme Commander's case that what he calls a "major involvement," implying failure to impose the pause for deliberation, would "bring into operation the full efforts of all the forces and factors that make up the deterrent throughout the world." If aggression in its heaviest form, including the use of nuclear weapons, is not a major involvement, then what is? Yet, here is a perfectly clear statement that it is the job of the shield forces to deal with it.

It may be that this section quoted from General Norstad's speech had political undertones and was designed to bring comfort to the people living in the easternmost territories of the Alliance. But it seems to me a doubtful policy to extend such reassurance unless one is quite sure of the resources to fulfill it.

What is the real function of the shield? The Atlantic Council must surely make up its collective mind on the answer to this vital question. Is it to enforce a pause and, if necessary, subsequently fight a delaying action while the sword takes effect? Or is it to wage a major campaign with thousand-mile–range nuclear weapons on the eastern outpost line of the Alliance? And if it is the latter, where does the sword enter the picture? If the proper function of the shield is accepted to be what the Supreme Commander described to the NATO Parliamentarians as bridging the gap between all or nothing—which can only mean between peace and a situation in which the aggressor has clearly made his conscious choice for all-out war—then one can obviously agree. But that is something quite different from defending Europe against "aggression in its heaviest form."

In my own view, the true function of the shield forces is, first, that described by General Norstad as their basic objective—enforcing the pause, which in itself involves stamping promptly and effectively on the "incident," smothering the small outbreak of fire before it spreads into a conflagration. If that fails—if the enemy makes his conscious choice for "unmistakable, deliberate, all-out aggression"—then the shield's function is to act as a covering and delaying force to stem the invasion until the strategic force can take effective action.

My conception of the basic objectives of strategy in Europe is probably not as far from General Norstad's as it may appear. I believe that the battle force can be much more than just a rear guard falling back before the surge of enemy armor to the Channel coast—but only if it is reinforced with more striking capacity, reorganized, and re-equipped. It is important, though, to set the record straight in two respects.

First, the initial operations to enforce the pause must be planned, and the necessary troops must be organized, equipped, and trained specifically for that purpose. Nuclear weapons are the last things that would be required for this role; nor could there be any question at this stage of "taking out" enemy airfields or rail centers by air attack, nuclear or otherwise. One of the certainties of any future war is that once we or the enemy started using nuclear weapons against objectives like these, deep in enemy-controlled territory, then there would be no hope of avoiding unlimited escalation; it would, in fact, precipitate the general nuclear exchange that at this stage it would be the whole object of the covering force to prevent. The striking element of the battle force would have to be poised, ready for instant action—but not used. Once the real battle were joined, once the enemy had made his deliberate choice of all-out action, then we would take him on with every weapon in our armory. If it comes to that, I see no reason for undue pessimism about our chances for success—except that a victory for either side would be decidedly Pyrrhic. But the point is that the initial task is simply to enforce the pause *and nothing else*—to present the enemy with the dilemma of option for settlement by negotiation or all-out war, and to give him every opportunity to choose the former and no excuse not to do so.

The second point is that it would be quite wrong to leave anybody—least of all the enemy—with the impression that the battle force could or would attempt to defend Europe against "aggression in its heaviest form" without invoking the use of the strategic force. That would certainly be impossible—and it also must be unmistakably clear to the Kremlin leaders that if they decide on all-out aggression in any form, theirs will be the responsibility for unleashing the terrible fury of nuclear war, that if they try to kill us, they will themselves be killed. It is an utter delusion to imagine that a major war could be fought in the second half of the twentieth century in a conventional, noncatastrophic manner, even if the democracies were willing and able to raise and maintain in peacetime the forces that would be required —which they obviously are not (and for excellent reasons).

There is one further point in General Norstad's exposition that I think needs clarifying: his reference to the need for his forces to be sufficiently versatile to deal with any form of attack, with the implication that they must be able to switch at short notice from conventional to nuclear operations. This seems to me (and to many experienced army officers) to have pronounced limitations. For reasons less connected with tactics or training than with logistics and the organization of lines of communication and supply, I do not believe a great army like Land Forces Central Europe could fight a conventional war from, say, D-day to D-plus-7 and then suddenly switch to a nuclear one. As long as we clearly do not expect them to, I am not as concerned as some by the fact that the five excellent American divisions in Germany—and, to an increasing extent, the British Army of the Rhine—would be unable to fight except with nuclear weapons. They would have their own role to play, but not in the covering force.

I have suggested that the striking units of the battle force should be increased in numbers and power. I do not think that is necessary for the land units. The real requirement is for reorganization and re-equipment of those we have, in accordance with their tactical role in battle. Indeed, I believe that if this were done, we could even manage with fewer numbers than we shall have when German rearmament is complete.

What, then, should be the composition and shape of the battle force of the Alliance in Europe?

First, there must be the *covering force*—the screen on the frontiers, the forces to deal promptly with "incidents" (if the Communists mean business, we must assume that they would stage more than one simultaneously). In my view, if an incident assumed proportions that could not be handled by, at most, two or three brigade groups (regimental combat teams), we should be perilously near the point of failure in the effort to enforce the pause. No one would be so foolish as to suggest a purely linear defense along the frontier, though there must be forward detachments in close contact with the frontier police in order to give immediate warning and deal promptly with any petty infiltration. To this extent, we need, not the conventional kind of forward strategy, but a partition-line strategy.

What we must have in order to deal with the incident is a number of highly mobile groups at fire-brigade readiness, available for movement at once (literally, within a matter of hours) to the threatened point or points. We should be able to have on the spot within twelve hours a brigade group, air-dropped or air-transported, consisting of regular troops with only light artillery, but carefully trained in riot duties and guerrilla-type operations, including street fighting. This should be kept in instant readiness, probably as a "duty brigade" on a roster, since it is too much to expect the whole covering force to be maintained permanently in peacetime at such a standard. And we should be able to follow it up immediately with another, similar brigade, but moved by land in its own transport vehicles, and with some armor. The covering force need not and should not have nuclear weapons.

Three or four covering groups of this nature, suitably disposed along the front and with air transport available to move them, would be enough to deal promptly with incidents. The essence is mobility, readiness, and the right kind of training.

But we must be able to reinforce them, if necessary, with heavier forces—to have on the spot, within a matter of days, a support group from the "main force," which should include battlefield nuclear weapons and have its own quota of reconnaissance aircraft. The mere movement and presence of such a group might well call a halt to the proceedings, since it would be a clear indication that we meant business. If it did not, then the pause would merge into the battle, and the task of both the covering and main forces would become normal defense and delaying actions (if one can describe any kind of nuclear war as "normal"). At this point, the *striking force* and the *strategic force* would both have been fully alerted.

The entire battle area would, of course, have to be covered by the *NATO air defense force*—consisting of fighters, equipped with air-to-air nuclear weapons, and surface-to-air guided weapons, served by the necessary control and early warning system.

I do not propose to go into any detail about the strength of these forces. It is the principle that I want to emphasize; the details must be settled by those with the responsibility. Suffice it to say that I believe the forces could be found without putting an unacceptable burden on Western resources. It is not so much a question of numbers as of organization, equipment, training, and, above all, a clear conception of what the battle force is required to do.

There is, however, a way in which the numbers and resisting power of the regular forces can be valuably supplemented at relatively little cost. The defense of Europe is, in the first instance, primarily a question of the defense of Germany. Thus, it seems to me that the covering force should be drawn from the twelve divisions of the new German Army. But in its battle role, it and the main force should be supplemented by a new German "territorial citizen force," comprising young and middle-aged men who have received their training in World War II or as conscripts in the regular army. In an earlier book, I suggested that a network of such local units (with members who were thoroughly familiar with every inch of their own ground) could constitute a formidable supplementary obstacle to invasion.* Their duties would include antitank defense, demolitions, and emergency backing of the frontier police for internal-security purposes in the forward area. Being only semimobile, with locally requisitioned means of transport, they could have no strategic offensive capacity and would be less vulnerable to nuclear weapons than regular formations with their great masses of transport and supporting weapons.

One word about the striking element of the battle force, which should comprise all bomber and fighter-bomber aircraft and missiles—in fact, all weapons other than conventional and battlefield nuclear ones. If the responsible authorities consider that the existing striking capacity available to the Supreme Commander is inadequate (and I would be inclined to agree with them), then it must be increased. And, in practice, it can only be increased at the expense of the strategic forces. In my view, this should be a function

---

* *Strategy for the West*, pp. 77–78.

of the RAF Bomber Command—especially since, for at least the next decade, the requirement of the battle force will be more for manned aircraft, including the new types specifically designed for low-level operation, than for missiles. The striking force would include, of course, the present tactical air forces, as well as German units.

It is true that Bomber Command is now an important component of the Allied strategic forces. But these forces would already possess a material "overkill" capacity if all their units were appropriately distributed. The major contribution of Bomber Command to the strength and diversity of Western strategic capacity lies in the fact that "it increases dispersal and reduces reaction time."* If the Command were assigned to the NATO battle force, its loss to the strategic forces could be compensated for by a redeployment of the American Strategic Air Command, with a higher proportion of its strength based on the eastern side of the Atlantic, and by the increasing number of Polaris submarines.

Here, then, is my proposed new makeup of the present shield forces under the Supreme Commander in Europe: the covering force, without nuclear arms, to deal with the initial incident; backed by the main force, armed with battlefield nuclear weapons; both to act in a holding and delaying role in the event of failure to enforce the pause; both supplemented in this role by the German territorial force; all covered by the air defense force and supported by an augmented striking force. Surely, if this conception were adopted, there would be no need to darken counsel by talking about a NATO deterrent or turning NATO into a fourth nuclear power.

* *Report on Defence.*

Chapter 8

First Steps Toward Arms Control and Political Adjustment in Europe

AN IMPORTANT ADVANTAGE of a military reorganization along the lines just suggested is that, as well as corresponding more closely with military reality, the proposed new make-up of the forces in Europe lends itself most conveniently to what I now wish to propose as the first stage of arms control and political adjustment in Europe. Briefly, my plan is as follows:

The covering force and elements of the air defense force (and, naturally, of the German territorial network) must be located well forward in Germany during peacetime, ready to deploy at the shortest notice in an emergency. So also must a part of the main force; its German components would have to be stationed in Germany anyway, but it is not essential that the entire main force should be, since there would be time for a concentration of the whole forward after the initial incident.

The striking force, on the other hand, need not—and, indeed, should not—be stationed on German soil. I think this could lead to the withdrawal of corresponding Russian units from the soil of East Germany, though I would not make that a condition. As an example set by us, it might well result in pressure upon the Kremlin leaders by their allies in the Warsaw Pact, including the East Germans, to follow it; none of these satellites can welcome the presence on its soil of targets that would inevitably attract nuclear attack in the event of battle. At any rate, it has the advantage of being a measure of arms control in which a start can be made without first securing Russian agreement. It would not, in practice, involve any genuine handicap for our side, because I do not believe that air units of the striking force could, in any event, be maintained at forward airfields in Germany in battle, while missiles could be deployed west of the Rhineland frontier and still be able to perform their function in battle, with those on mobile mountings being moved forward if and when necessary. For the same reason, I am not dismayed by the argument often advanced against redeployment: that it would mean giving up all the expensive tactical air bases in Germany, vast concrete runways and aprons that are, in fact, the antithesis of the word "tactical," implying as it does flexibility and mobility. Actually, they would be useful in peace and in the opening phase before battle for the transport and reconnaissance aircraft of the covering force and for forward elements of the air defense force. But once real battle began, they would be useless; it is impossible to believe that most of them would not be wiped out at once by nuclear attack. This, of course, is the prime reason for the rapid development of aircraft of all classes with short and vertical take-off and landing characteristics, capable of operation from any reasonably level pasture or highway.

It may be asked why, in this case, the proposal is considered of any value as a measure of arms control. I have already suggested one answer. But I think it would also have some value as a first step in reducing the fear of surprise attack. This is very largely a psychological matter; and in this sense, I believe it would have an important effect on the minds of the German population on our side, who are already evincing some anxiety about all these nuclear targets in their midst. On the Communist side, there would be not only the parallel effect already referred to, but also that of knowing that at least the German units in the front line against them—those of the covering force—were not nuclear-armed; while the semistatic territorial force could not be regarded as a genuine menace to the satellite states, let alone the Soviet Union.

This may not appear to be very much, but it would at least be a beginning, and we must make a start somewhere.

However, while announcing this as our policy and beginning to put it into effect, at the same time we should put to the Russians a proposal that could have much more far-reaching results, but one that obviously could not be initiated without their agreement. I have already stressed the fact that effective control and inspection must be a *sine qua non* of any real measure of disarmament, and I have repeatedly urged the virtues of gradualness. Once we have made a start, our aim must be control and inspection of all weapons with which either side could attack the other, including the strategic units on Russian and Western soil, pending their ultimate abolition. But I have also pointed out that if we go too far in our initial demands for a comprehensive scheme of control and inspection, we shall never even make the start. Something is better than nothing, and we should begin in a small way in an area in which it may well suit the Russians to do something effective, and where we have at least the propaganda advantage that the Kremlin has repeatedly in recent years made a variety of relevant proposals of varying degrees of dishonesty.* In any event, even if comprehensive inspection were agreed upon, it would be a very long time before it could be put into effect, and we would still have to make a modest beginning in a limited zone.

The proposal is that Germany, East and West together, should become—by gradual, limited stages—a pilot, prototype area, in which the armaments, deployment, and strengths of the opposing forces would be subject to verified limitation and ultimate reduction, under a system of control and inspection by representatives of NATO and the Warsaw Pact acting in combination.

The first step should be the establishment of relatively narrow belts of radar early-warning and mobile ground control teams, manned by NATO on the Eastern frontier and by the Warsaw Pact nations on the Western frontier. These would remain permanently as tangible pledges of great-power commitment in the event of aggression from either side. Once this were established and proved, the second stage would be to extend it—if necessary again, by limited phases—to a zone of control and inspection covering all Germany. And the final stage, if and when this has been shown to work and some measure of confidence has been established, would be the thinning out and eventual withdrawal of all forces except German ones from the soil of Germany. The position of Berlin would have to be reserved for special treatment, perhaps under U.N. supervision, until danger to the integrity of that city were removed.

---

* See E. Hinterhoff, *Disengagement* (London: Atlantic Books, 1959), Appendix 10.

The whole process might well take ten years; and it would then have to be underwritten by some form of mutual-security undertaking, of which an essential feature must be the long-term commitment of Britain and America to the defense of Germany.

To the more ardent advocates of disarmament and disengagement, such a proposal may appear inadequate. To me, it seems ambitious enough to merit a serious effort. It involves risks, but surely no more than does an indefinite prolongation of the status quo. It will not afford complete protection against surprise attack; but, again, it is certainly better than nothing, and I do not believe we shall get anywhere except by a strategy of limited objectives.

There is little point in my elaborating on this proposal; once the principle were accepted, the details would obviously have to be worked out with great care and precision by the responsible authorities. Let us not confuse the issue by looking too far ahead, worrying about such remote questions as whether East Germany should ultimately become a demilitarized zone; whether West Germany should ultimately withdraw from NATO and become militarily nonaligned, like Sweden; or just how, when, and to where Allied forces should be withdrawn if the time comes. These matters must all be considered and decided in due course. But let us take first things first, get the principle accepted and make a start, leaving the rest to be worked out as the plan develops. In putting forward a similar plan in 1954, I suggested that we should announce our intention, once the new German forces were fully operational, of withdrawing British, American, and French forces from the German Federal Republic whether or not the Russians at the same time withdrew their troops from East Germany. I still think it is an idea that at least should not be ruled out in advance; but, again, this is something that can be considered at a later stage, when we can judge the progress of events.

This proposal does, of course, ultimately involve what I regretfully accept must continue to be known as "disengagement." I dislike the term: partly because it suggests a military vacuum in Central Europe, which makes no sense; and partly because it has come to convey a connotation in some quarters that I, as one of its early protagonists, never intended—something that could safely be done quickly, without proper safeguards, perhaps through a summit meeting. Maybe the idea was too attractive, seeming to imply that we could "bring the boys home" and all live happily ever after.

Disengagement has been interpreted as involving something else that was never intended—the withdrawal of American power from Europe within the foreseeable future. Field Marshal Montgomery, for instance, asked in an article in *The Sunday Times* (March 29, 1959), "Why not let all national forces withdraw to their own countries?" He did go on to say that this could not be completed "until the European security problem is solved," though he did not explain what he meant by his condition. He also said that "such action involves no question of disengagement," which I imagine was his way of saying it could not involve a military vacuum. And he has recently restated in a television interview that he "would like to see the armed forces of the two blocs withdraw from Europe to their own territories," though it should be done gradually. On this occasion, he gravely oversimplified a highly difficult and complex question by saying that the Americans should so organize their armed forces that they could get back to Europe "very quickly"—that they should have ten or twelve divisions with enough air transport to enable them "to be sent anywhere at twelve hours' notice." The Field Marshal should surely know that the present U.S. military air transport resources would be hard put to it to handle one division over the distances involved.

It cannot be too often or too emphatically said that an American military presence on the eastern side of the Atlantic will be an essential condition of European security for as far ahead as anyone need now look. This does not necessarily mean the full five divisions now in Germany; but it does mean some strong, highly mobile, nuclear-armed land forces, as well as contingents of the U.S. Air Force and the nuclear-armed carriers and submarines in European waters. If and when the thinning out of other than German forces begins, the French and British should be the first to withdraw. And when her turn comes, the United States must retain powerful elements in Great Britain, on the Continent, and in North Africa if that is still possible, with the sea and air transport to get them back quickly (quite a different matter from moving ten or twelve divisions across the Atlantic on twelve hours' notice) and with stockpiles of heavy equipment stored on Continental soil.

Finally, on this matter of disengagement, I do not consider my proposal as in any way making a dangerous concession to the Russians. On the contrary, despite their past protestations, we should probably have great difficulty in getting them to accept it. I think it contains advantages for both sides. But if it reached the stage of serious negotiations, the Russians would probably be very nervous about it, because of their view—however unreasonable it may be—of East Germany as a defensive glacis against possible attack from the West. A beguiling characteristic of criticism of disengagement as a policy is that it is almost equally divided between those who say it would be so dangerous for us that we should never suggest it, and others who claim that it would be so disastrous for the Russians that they would never accept it. Listening to some critics, one would almost imagine that the real object of our policy should be to keep the Red Army on the Elbe, at practically any cost.

I want to comment briefly on the problem of higher direction and command—first on the highest level, and then in Europe, with particular reference to the decision to use nuclear weapons. If it is true that the strategic concept governing the action of the forces in Europe has become blurred and confused, it is not the fault of General Norstad, an outstandingly able officer who has struggled manfully with problems and responsibilities that should not be his. The fault lies at the highest level, with the Atlantic Council and with the body from which it should draw its military advice and which should draft the strategic directives for its approval, the Standing Group. If, as I believe to be the case, the Standing Group has in recent years been sadly reduced in status and authority, that again is the fault of the Atlantic Council, which should never have allowed it to happen. It is fantastic to imagine that wise, consistent, dynamic military policy can possibly emerge from a body representing fifteen national chiefs of staff. The first thing to do is to restore the authority of the Standing Group, make it a "super chief of staff in commission," and insist on its resuming its former function of strategic advice, acting always in consultation with the Military Committee, but not subordinate to it. From my personal experience of the Standing Group, I can see no serious objection to its comprising four members. The position of Germany as the strongest land power in NATO must be recognized, and General Heusinger is an admirable candidate to represent his country in the group.

The difficulty on the lower level about deciding when to use nuclear weapons is a real one, but perhaps not as serious as has been imagined. Among democracies, the decision cannot and should not be left to the soldier in a matter that may involve the life or death of nations. With all due respect, I do not think Prime Minister Macmillan's "fifteen fingers on the safety catch" is a very real difficulty; there will be more than fifteen reaching for the safety catch when it comes to that point, whatever the constitutional system of responsibility. The decision is not one that can be made by fifteen ambassadors or ministers around a table; I know of few decisions that are. I think the solution probably lies in some sort of political "standing group" of three or four to which the others, whether they liked it or not, would have to delegate responsibility.

But my point here is to suggest that if and when the time came, the problem would not really be as difficult as it sometimes appears. This is an issue that itself would be somewhat simplified by my proposed reorganization of the battle force. And if my picture of how the situation would develop is at all valid, then it seems clear that it would not be a matter of three or four harassed and tired men going into a last-minute huddle. There would be time—a matter of days, at least—for measured assessment of the situation, for consultation with other allies, and for making the decision that, in point of fact, would almost inevitably force itself upon them through the stress of circumstances.

Finally, the Atlantic Council should take a very careful look at the system of command in Europe. I am very doubtful that it makes sense for one man to try to exercise command over a front stretching from the North Cape to the Tabriz gap. And, especially if we strengthen the striking force, I find it difficult to believe that one unfortunate individual at Marly could exercise more than nominal control over the land-air battles on that vast front and at the same time direct an air and missile counteroffensive a thousand miles into hostile territory. I am inclined to think the solution is to have two separate commands, one the present Allied Forces Central and Northern Europe (which must be locked together) and the other the present Allied Forces Southern Europe and Mediterranean. The higher direction could be exercised by the suggested new political and the existing military standing groups, along lines similar to those followed by the Prime Minister and President with the Combined Chiefs of Staff in World War II. And there is no reason why there should not be a NATO reserve of air forces and air-transportable land forces under central control, available to reinforce either front as required.

Indeed, some system of coordination would be essential, particularly among the striking forces, which might have to be combined under a central air force commander serving both fronts (something like the Mediterranean Allied Tactical Air Force in 1944, which served both the Fifth and Eighth Armies in the Italian Campaign). In that case, the central striking force should include both the Sixth Fleet and any Polaris submarines assigned to NATO.

On the subject of strategy for Europe, there is one more relevant point that should be made. Some critics maintain that Great Britain should no longer devote any of her limited resources to what they quite misleadingly call an "independent" British deterrent, and that our contribution to NATO instead should consist of more and better conventional troops. At first sight, there is much force in this argument, which is at least based on reason rather than emotion—though I suspect it is sometimes not altogether free from electoral expediency and that most natural of human ambitions, the desire to have the best of both worlds. What is lacking in my view, is a sober and practical appraisal of military realities.

To begin with, the argument is founded on a fallacy—the idea that Bomber Command is an independent British deterrent and that its military value in relation to SAC is negligible, or at best marginal. As the White Paper (*Report on Defence*) repeatedly emphasizes, Bomber Command is the British "contribution to the strategic nuclear deterrent of the West," and its operational planning is closely tied in with that of SAC; moreover, far from being negligible, it is "an important element in the total power of the Western deterrent." It is important in two ways: first, that it "provides a valuable degree of strength and diversity to the Western forces as a whole. It increases dispersal and reduces reaction time." It is entirely misleading merely to count numbers of first-line aircraft and deduce that the military value of Bomber Command is in direct ratio to its numerical strength compared with SAC, thus ignoring important considerations of time and space—including the highly significant fact that Bomber Command is based several thousand miles nearer to its potential targets than is most of SAC.

Secondly, it is not too much to claim that the existence of a nuclear striking force on the British side of the Atlantic, and not under the exclusive control of the U.S. Government, might validate the Allied deterrent as a whole in certain circumstances. I will try briefly to explain a point that is not too far-fetched to represent a real addition to the influence of the Western deterrent. In the absence of Bomber Command, the Russians might be tempted to adopt Hitler's technique of picking off his enemies one by one. They might become convinced that if they attacked only Britain, telling the Americans that their quarrel was not with them, the United States might not be willing to accept the awful risks of all-out nuclear war. I do not believe for one moment that the United States would go back on her obligations in this way; but this hardly matters as much as what the Kremlin leaders think she would do. Dictators, generally with limited and often misleading information about the real attitudes of other countries, sometimes make very silly mistakes. Hitler did not really believe that Britain would fight in 1939—and still less that she would go on fighting alone when France fell. If the Kremlin did make that mistake about the United States, it would no doubt be rudely disillusioned—*but the war would already be on,* or at least events might have reached a stage from which it would be very difficult for the Kremlin to back down.

But in Bomber Command, we British have a striking force that, before it was wiped out (as no doubt it soon would be), could inflict appalling damage on Russia. The Kremlin could never be certain that the United States would not intervene—and that is a point of extreme importance in this entire matter of deterrence: It is not essential for the Russians to be sure that we *would* retaliate; what is vital is that they never become certain that we would *not*. And I cannot believe that they would be so sure as to accept the risk of finding themselves up against the unscathed might of the United States, after they had gone through the first round and emerged in a terribly crippled condition.

In other words, they must decide from the beginning to go all the way—to take on the United States with the rest— or not go to war at all. I have no doubt about what the decision would be. This does not mean that the object of Bomber Command is to "trigger off" SAC—an inane phrase that seems to indicate that a British Government would use Bomber Command to start a nuclear war and commit the United States against her will. I am getting at something totally different: that we should force the potential aggressor to face the necessity of attacking the United States as well as the British—with the result that he would not choose war.

I am not suggesting that any policy should be immutable or that Bomber Command would necessarily survive the final elimination of the manned bomber, which the 1961 *Report on Defence* properly implies is much further off than some people (including the author of the previous White Paper in 1957) seem to think. Our defense policy must be flexible and adaptable to changing circumstances. Nor do I claim that, if we had to start from scratch *now*, a nuclear air striking force would necessarily be the best British contribution to the combined strength of the West. I submit that herein lies the answer to those who say: But all the arguments apply equally to other NATO powers; why shouldn't the

French, as well as the British, have an "independent" bomber command? The answer is that there is no earthly reason why they should not if that is their most appropriate means of spending the enormous effort and resources involved. The point is that, unlike the British, neither France nor any other NATO power has a bomber command. With the best will in the world, the French, having no background of experience or expertise in the field, could not possibly build up a nuclear striking force equivalent in value even to Bomber Command in much less than ten years. Within that critical period, I think there are other ways in which the French, with their superb military qualities, could contribute better to the common defense than by laboriously building up from nothing a bomber command—or for that matter a carrier-based fleet air arm, another branch of the military art in which they have no special aptitude.

On the other hand, Bomber Command has been a leading element of the British defense establishment for a quarter-century. We have an invaluable background of war experience, of technical and tactical expertise—the United States having learned something from us about bombing as well as nuclear science.

To pull out of the business at this stage would thus seem the height of folly. It would take us years to build up any comparably valuable substitute for Bomber Command as a contribution to Western defense. Having just dispensed (by amalgamation) with a lot of good infantry, armored, and artillery units, are we now to start re-forming them all again, despite our doubtful ability to find enough volunteers to fill the ranks even of our present diminished army?

However nice such solutions may sound in theory, we really must consider the hard facts of life before presenting them as serious contributions to strategy.

Chapter 9

Global Strategy

"THE COMPLETE COLLAPSE of colonialism is imminent" according to the Moscow declaration, which made clear beyond doubt that peaceful coexistence is to include "a determined struggle . . . against imperialism and the remnants of feudalism" in Asia, Africa, and Latin America—the prime target, of course, being American imperialism. Here is a declaration of political, social, and economic war on a global scale, and it is on that scale that it must be met and defeated.

How such a campaign can be directed and its operations coordinated among the free nations of the West is a problem for which a solution is not easily found. Here again, it is less difficult for the monolithic Communist system, with its completely controlled economy and freedom from the trammels of accepted international procedures, to pursue the offensive than for the democracies to hold the fort. General de Gaulle is, no doubt, right in urging that there should be a global strategy for the free world as a whole—and he is not the first to have put forward that view.* Just how it is

* See Slessor, *The Great Deterrent*, p. 289.

to be done is a different matter. But one thing should be clear: It is not a task for NATO or for the other regional treaty organizations, CENTO and SEATO. It is primarily in the economic and political fields that this war must be waged; and to associate operations in these fields with military pacts is to condemn them in advance, especially since, for the most part, they have to be conducted with or in countries that are either neutral or at least militarily nonaligned. There has in recent years been much useful consultation in the Atlantic Council on matters far beyond the geographical boundaries of NATO that directly affect the Allied powers in their relations with each other; but nothing would more certainly wreck NATO than to try to turn the Council and its military staffs into a sort of global cabinet and general staff to direct the international affairs of the free world.

In the economic sphere, the task is less difficult than in the political—though, of course, the two are to some extent inevitably interdependent. The problems are still formidable and need more coordinated effort than yet exists; but there is a whole spectrum of institutions working actively on them—U.N. agencies, Commonwealth institutions, the Colombo Plan, the International Development Agency, the World Bank and International Monetary Fund—and cooperation will be carried still further in the near future with the establishment of the Organization for Economic Cooperation and Development. I have already hinted at the implications for our own economies and standards of living; I shall not attempt to elaborate further, except to make two points.

First, I repeat once more that this economic strategy should not be regarded primarily as war against Communism. We have in the past made too many mistakes by tying up economic aid with military strings—to say nothing of dispensing money in the attempt to win military allegiance.

This is a policy to be pursued in its own right, with wise discrimination and some self-sacrifice on the part of the wealthier nations, if we want to build a better world. Secondly, an indispensable counterpart of action on the economic front surely must be social action on the birth-rate front in the underdeveloped countries. Medical science has done wonders to reduce the numbers of people who die prematurely; no one has done enough to match that by reducing the numbers who are born. *Something* is being done: Few of us who knew India in the old days would have believed that "family planning" would become a policy of an Indian Government in our lifetime. But far more is necessary if economic cooperation is to do more than just keep pace with the rise in populations.

But economic development is not the whole story. Indeed, as George Kennan has reminded us in one of his Reith lectures, "Benevolence, if prolonged for any length of time, comes to be taken for granted as a right and its withdrawal resented as an injury"—and this becomes even more true when the recipients come to understand (as they must) that it is not merely benevolence but an enlightened form of self-interest.

In the sphere of international politics, action is more difficult to agree upon and coordinate among a number of free countries with widely different historical backgrounds, attitudes, and current interests and responsibilities. However, this is an area in which the "big three" of NATO are primarily concerned and must provide the lead, and it is easier for three nations to agree than for fifteen. Still, the three must always be careful to respect the interests and opinions of their smaller partners, especially those (like the Dutch) who have long experience and retain some responsibilities in overseas areas.

Of Great Britain's role: "The proper aim has been defined as that of becoming the Greeks in the new Roman Empire of

the United States. To achieve this position she needs to preserve above all a capital of respect for her wisdom, maturity,
moderation and skill, a capital well built up in the decade
that followed the end of the Second World War but then
wildly dissipated in the crazy gamble of Suez."* Much has
been done since 1956, through the patient statesmanship of
Mr. Macmillan, to redress the damage dealt by that inex-
plicable blunder (for which the blame must lie almost as
much with the so-called "diplomacy" of Mr. Dulles as with
Sir Anthony Eden's climactic misjudgment). There are also
sound reasons for hope that the major foreign-policy errors
of the United States during the eight years of the Eisenhower
Administration may be retrieved by the dynamic leadership
of President Kennedy and the wise judgment of Secretary of
State Dean Rusk. And in Paris, Charles de Gaulle, the man
who could go down in history as the greatest statesman of
the postwar generation, may succeed in dispelling at last the
somber cloud of frustration and defeat that has dimmed the
glory of France for twenty years.

Sir William Hayter tells us that in these days diplomacy
"operates not through gun-boats or their modern equivalents
but through patient negotiation [and] a scrupulous respect for
treaty obligations and treaty rights"—and he might have added
that this diplomacy is powerless unless those of us who observe the rules have the courage and ability to insist, in the
proper way and by legitimate means, that other people also
observe them. It will usually be true that the Communist
offensive in the uncommitted countries can best be met, not
by its own methods, but by wise and understanding diplomacy, by liberal and forward-looking racial policies, watch-
ful patience, and tolerance of behavior that in more mature
societies might be intolerable. We must help these emergent
states not only by economic assistance, but also by giving

---

* Sir William Hayter, *The Diplomacy of the Great Powers* (London:
Hamish Hamilton, 1960).

them time to learn the arts of government and international usage, by respecting the dignity of the individual (even if, as too often, he has little dignity), and by helping to build up an educated middle class, responsible politicians and administrators, and all the infrastructure of social institutions which go to form the foundations of any civilized state.

Nevertheless, we should make no mistake that this (as the Moscow declaration states), is a determined struggle, a Cold War in which Russia, having come up against the firm barrier of NATO in Europe, is following her traditional technique of finding soft spots on unguarded flanks. There is a limit to the extent to which we can play the game according to the rules, when our opponent insists on playing it outside them. The Communists light and fan the fires of active rebellion and keep them stoked by the supply of arms, aircraft, "advisers,"—and sometimes even active "volunteers." But when the West attempts to support the local people who resist the Communists, they invoke the claims of national sovereignty (habitually ignored when it suits their purposes), opening the floodgates of vitriolic abuse and threats about what will happen to the "imperialists" who dare to protect their own interests or those of their friends. We have seen several examples of this in recent years.

I have already suggested that we should treat such threats with the contempt they deserve. We should never lose our tempers and be stampeded into impetuous action. But a time may come—after every resource of political action and diplomacy, including those available through the United Nations, has been tried and has failed—when our only alternative to being "nibbled to death" will be to use collective force. If we are never prepared to do that, if we are law-abiding to the extreme logical conclusion in a world that still, for the most part, ultimately respects only strength and pays little attention to law except when its observance is expedient—then we are lost.

I do not propose to discuss here the strategy of limited warfare, a subject that would require a book in itself. Actually, the kind of operations with which we may be faced will not, as a rule, be in the category even of *limited* war. They will be more akin to what, in unregenerate days, we British used to call "imperial policing." And here, as on the partition line in Europe, prompt and resolute action to stamp out the small brushfire will usually prevent it from becoming a serious conflagration. Too often, we have seen situations in which a division was needed by the end of a year to deal with an outbreak that could have been stamped out in a month by a battalion if it had been there in time.

But we cannot be sure that such operations will not amount to more than that, and the essential point is that we should never be deterred from resolute collective action by the fear of provoking Russia to the point of major war. The deterrent exists not only to deter an aggressor from undertaking total war as an instrument of policy, but also (and of more frequent practical importance) to enable us to undertake such political and—in the last resort—military actions as may be required to protect our interests and our friends, and to enable the new nations to develop in freedom, without being inhibited by the fear of total war. Nuclear blackmail is a favorite gambit of the Kremlin's in these circumstances. It loses all validity if we treat it as what it is—a colossal and impertinent bluff.

There are, however, some essential conditions that must be observed in undertaking military operations on any scale larger than mere brushfire police action. The first is that there can be no question of "going it alone." When possible, of course, we should obtain United Nations sanction for any action. But we know that this is not something we can always count on, and we should not necessarily be inhibited by opposition in an Assembly that includes such manifestly "impartial" new nations as Guinea and Yemen. But we must take into account the interests of NATO and our allies in that and other regional treaties. We must be sure in advance that we shall at least not incur the opposition of our allies or of other Commonwealth countries—though we cannot expect all of them to sympathize with us always. We certainly cannot expect the active cooperation of all our associates in every case. But we are at least entitled to expect that they would back us up—*provided* we at least inform them and, if possible, consult them well in advance.

There are other important conditions to be observed in such circumstances: All the resources of economic, political, and diplomatic action must first be exhausted; the reasons for our action should be unmistakably valid and clear; the object of the specific military action involved, and its reasonably foreseeable results, should be commensurate with its broader political and strategic implications; the timing should be right; and finally, of course, the military methods adopted must be swift and effective, and must be carried through to the required conclusion.

The last condition requires the existence in adequate strength of the right sort of troops with, above all, the necessary mobility. Their numbers need not be great, especially since it is difficult to envisage circumstances in which localized military action could be carried out on anything but a collective basis. The main essential is that they be appropriately trained and equipped and able to reach their destination quickly. The provisions now being made for up-to-date assault ships and landing craft should prove helpful. One of our disadvantages, as compared with the Communist bloc, is that all the probable areas of localized, limited war are so located that our forces must reach them from overseas—though this also has some disadvantages for the Communists, provided we have the resolution to exploit them. Military air transport—though its resources must be and are being increased—may not be enough in all circumstances: The political air barrier across the Middle East, for example, is now an inconvenient fact of life. Our geographical handicaps—the fact, for instance, that the cheapest and in some other ways most suitable peacetime stations for the bulk of the U.S. and British strategic reserves are in America and Great Britain—can be (and are being) reduced by maintaining limited reserves and stockpiles of heavy equipment at suitable strategic centers overseas. Nevertheless, adequate sea and air transport and vessels of the commando-carrier type are required to give them the necessary mobility. We have recently seen more than one example of how these strategic stockpiles tend to vanish or not to be in the place where they are wanted.

Are we, however, quite sure that the troops of our strategic reserves are being appropriately trained and equipped for these localized, limited wars? The need for them to be acclimatized and trained for the varying conditions of desert and jungle warfare—a lesson learned at great cost in World War II—is recognized; the British have desert and jungle training areas in North Africa and Malaya, the French have certainly had as much practice as they need in guerrilla warfare in Algeria, and the United States has within its own borders ample desert and tropical areas for training. But it seems possible to me that the training and equipment of our reserve formations may be unduly influenced by the conditions of major European warfare. The sort of formation required for that purpose, with its masses of armor and dependence on motorized transport, is not suitable for limited operations in desert or tropical country (in fact, it may not even be as suitable as some people think for war in Europe). No doubt some armor might be required. But we have ample proof that the American or British soldier can be just as tough and can be trained to be just as desert- or jungle-wise as any Arab or Japanese. My own personal memories of small wars in Africa and on the old Indian frontier make me feel that we should be wise to take as a model for the training of the infantry in our strategic reserves something akin to the old Pathan irregular militias, who went cheerfully to war with a rifle and bandolier, a water bottle, and a bag of very austere rations—and thought little of doing thirty or forty miles a day over frontier country on their hard, flat feet.

The question arises as to whether nuclear weapons should —or might ever have to be—used in these limited wars. It seems impossible to give a generalized negative answer. We would be very unwise to commit ourselves in advance to an unqualified undertaking not to use them in any circumstances. They should certainly not be used except as a last resort, when nothing else could save us from failure to achieve the object for which we have gone to war—and we should not embark on any operations unless we have faced the ultimate possibility of having to go to any lengths necessary to ensure their success. The governing principle is the traditional one (now disguised by elaborate terms such as "graduated deterrence") that in any military situation one must use the degree of force required to achieve one's object—no more, and certainly no less.

Underlying peoples' doubts on this score, there is obviously the fear that even the use of the relatively small though still deadly battlefield nuclear weapon would lead to unlimited escalation. I do not share this anxiety in the circumstances we are now considering, although, let me repeat, I think these weapons should only be used as a last resort. It is not (within the obvious limits of reason) the use of any particular weapon that will determine whether or not the war remains limited, but the *issue at stake*—whether either side (not necessarily the actual combatants, but their principal supporters) can afford to admit failure. And in this respect, we probably have the advantage, since it is difficult to foresee any such situation in which the Kremlin would not consider failure (which they would no doubt regard as a purely temporary setback) to

achieve their end in one of these localized conflicts as preferable to the risk of total war. I feel less certain on this score
regarding Peking—reason enough for us to tread very cau-
tiously in our Far Eastern policy.

Let us take a hypothetical example. Suppose the West were
compelled to intervene to preserve the integrity of Israel
against an Arab attack inspired and incited by Moscow. Suppose, further, that a situation arose in which we were in danger of defeat. Is it suggested that our use of a tactical nuclear
bomb or shell against an Arab column in the desert would
result in the Russians' dropping a hydrogen bomb on, say,
Ankara or London or New York? Of course not. It might
conceivably mean that they would furnish the Egyptians with
a bomb to drop on Jerusalem; but in that event, what about
Cairo or Baghdad? It is surely important to view this sort of
problem in the proper perspective. It has often seemed curious to me that the people who are most vocal about the perils
of the Nth-power problem, who see alarming implications
in the possibility of someone like Nasser getting the bomb,
are so often the same people who protest that our own nuclear
capacity is useless as a deterrent because the British Government would never dare use it.

In a similar vein, we should not be too timid or allow legal
restrictions to stop us from taking the necessary action to
prevent the actions of Russia, either directly or through her
satellites, that fan the flames of local disorder or otherwise
create trouble for the West by the supply of arms to our ill-
wishers all over the world. Sometimes, we manifestly cannot
prevent it, as in Laos. But sometimes we could. Can anyone
imagine Khrushchev sitting quietly by while we supplied arms
to, say, Rumania? Why should we do nothing about Com-
munist-supplied guns being installed on the Bab el Mandeb?
Should we have done nothing to prevent Communist arms
from being poured into Indonesia, arms to be used to attack
Dutch New Guinea? If a new little nation like the Sudan can

prevent Khrushchev and Nasser from sending arms to their agents in the Congo—as it did—why cannot great powers like Britain and America do likewise? Does anyone seriously imagine that the Russian reaction would involve the risk of total war?

As long as we cannot bring ourselves to understand that the Russians have no intention of carrying matters to such an extreme, we shall presumably continue to allow our freedom of action to be paralyzed—to the immense advantage of international Communism.

Much has happened since the late Mr. Dulles made his pronouncement that neutrality was immoral. It is true that the world can broadly be divided into people who favor Communism and those who do not—and in that sense, he who is not with us is against us. But there is, in fact, a good deal to be said for neutrality, or at least for military nonalignment. It leaves us more flexibility of action. Most of the uncommitted countries would be of doubtful military value as allies (sometimes more of a liability than an asset); and the arms with which we would have to supply them at our expense might, in many cases, be used irresponsibly or for undesirable purposes. Some of these uncommitted nations enjoy the luxury of neutrality—and of treating us to moral homilies on the evils of militarism—secure in the belief that if they were really threatened, they could count on our support anyway, a belief that not all of them should be too sure is justified.

It is generally true that, to them, the gravest danger of Communism lies in the poverty and internal instability on which it feeds; and as a rule, their resources can be better utilized in rectifying that state of affairs than in building up armed forces that would be of very limited value to them if they were seriously attacked. Where I think we have some genuine cause for resentment is in their tendency to have the best of both worlds, to be so often "neutral against us"—

while enjoying all the advantages of Commonwealth membership, to take sides (regardless of the merits of the case and of whether or not colonialism is remotely relevant to the issue) with any so-called "anticolonialist" who may be embarrassing us. This is a form of indulgence to which Dr. Nkrumah is somewhat prone. We may smile tolerantly at his more picayune absurdities such as erecting statues of himself and putting his portrait on the Ghana coinage; even if we had any right to, we should not protest at his somewhat elastic interpretation of the term "democracy"; we are only too happy for him to be neutral in the Cold War if he wants to be. But the time may come, if he carries his pan-African ambitions too far, when he will have to choose between them and Commonwealth membership; the choice will be his—but so will the major loss.

Nor is that other, far greater, and more civilized Commonwealth country India altogether innocent of this unduly flexible interpretation of nonalignment. What, for instance, is one to think when Mr. Nehru, having clearly stated the conditions he thinks should be created in the Congo, within a week allows his representative in the United Nations to take a leading part in the defeat of a resolution that would have had the effect of enabling the Secretary General to create those very conditions? What other answer can there be but that the resolution of December 20, 1960, was sponsored by the two leading NATO powers, Britain and America, and that the Congo is a former Belgian colony. If this be either neutrality or statesmanship, it is surely a curious example.

What, then, can be done about these confused and contradictory emotions of people in the emergent countries? That wise observer George Kennan feels that "there is very little . . . over the short term, except to relax, to keep our composure, to refuse to be frightened by the Communist alternative, to refrain from doing the things that make matters worse and to let things come to rest, as in the end they must, on the sense of self-interest of the peoples concerned." I am sure that he would not exclude from this either the exercise of patient political diplomacy or cooperation in economic development free from military ties. We certainly should not discourage real neutrality. Mr. Kennan is obviously right when he says, "Until we learn better how to live without some of these people, we shall find it hard to live with them."* We should not be too impressed by their not uncommon attempts to use their uncommitted position between East and West as a bargaining point to influence our policy. I do not suggest that we should go so far as to say to them in effect: "All right, if you want to go Communist, then go Communist and see how you like it." But our attitude should sometimes be closer to that than it has been in the past. There is nonnuclear, as well as nuclear, blackmail—a tyranny of weakness, as well as of strength. We should submit to neither.

---

* Fifth Reith Lecture, December, 1957.

Chapter 10

Colonialism —
The American Obsession

BEFORE I GO ON to examine briefly some specific areas of "cold" conflict outside Europe, it seems necessary to speak frankly of one factor that for years has been a dangerously divisive influence in the relations between the United States and her allies in their dealings with the peoples of Asia and Africa.

The Moscow declaration included the usual expression of solidarity with "the peoples of Asia, Africa, Latin America, and Oceania who are carrying on a heroic struggle against imperialism," forecast the imminent breakdown of the system of colonial "slavery," etc.—the same mixture as before. This solidarity is largely mythical; the Soviets habitually use the frustrations and discontents in the less politically developed countries as instruments to further their own ends. However, it is unfortunately true that ever since the fighting ended in 1945, there has been little solidarity among the nations of the Western world in their policies toward the peoples of these vitally important areas. And this has been due, to a dangerous extent, to one factor.

Few things do more harm to the unity of the Atlantic Alliance and nothing irritates the friends of America more than the "holier-than-thou" attitude of most Americans and of successive U.S. administrations toward colonialism, whether of the British, French, Dutch, or Portuguese variety (though British colonialism does seem to have a special aura of wickedness in American eyes). A cardinal feature of the Communists' policy of peaceful coexistence is to divide and create antagonisms among the peoples of the West; and this American anticolonial obsession is an instrument on which they play consistently and cleverly, and unfortunately all too successfully. The exploitation of anticolonial sentiment, stirring up rebellion in the backward countries of Asia and Africa under the guise of liberation of oppressed colonial peoples, is one of the oldest tactics of Communist underground warfare, dating back to Lenin's earliest days; and somehow the Soviets manage to blandly disregard the fact that Russia is, and has been for generations, a far more brutally repressive colonial power than Britain or America has ever been. We have seen this offensive in action from Korea to Indochina, from Suez to Cyprus, in Malaya and Algeria, in Iraq and Syria—and most recently in the Congo. In all these places, it has found support and nourishment in the oldest American tribal myth. And the coming years will be replete with further similar opportunities for creating trouble and undermining the unity of the West.

There is, of course, nothing new about this American obsession. To go back no further than World War II, at a time when Winston Churchill was saying, "I have not become the King's first Minister in order to preside over the dissolution of the British Empire," his great colleague and ally in the White House was bending some of his energies to just that end. Englishmen acknowledge their indebtedness

to the man who gave us such valuable aid and encouragement even before Japanese folly forced his country into the
war on our side. But it would be amusing, were it not so
pathetically tragic, to remember that Mr. Roosevelt went to
Yalta imagining that he could get along with "Uncle Joe"
because Russia, unlike Great Britain, had no imperialist tradi-
tions or ambitions. One sometimes wishes that politicians
would read more of history. It is just as well that no English-
man knew at the time that Roosevelt was telling Stalin
privately behind Churchill's back that the British colony of
Hong Kong should be given back to China or international-
ized as a free port after the war. Perhaps the latter solution
might be a good one even now; but I wonder what the
American reaction would have been if Churchill had suggested privately to Stalin that Puerto Rico should be returned
to Spain.

Her anticolonial obsession has dogged and bedeviled
America's relations and cooperation with some of her most
loyal and valuable allies ever since the war. A classic example was the Suez affair. One of the worst blunders of the
Eisenhower Administration in that affair—blunders that on
the whole exceeded and to some extent caused the ultimate
folly of the Eden Government—was a statement made by
the late John Foster Dulles in a press conference in October,
1956. At a particularly delicate stage of the negotiations,
he announced that the United States was not able to identify
itself "100 per cent either with the colonial powers or with
the powers which are primarily and uniquely [*sic*] concerned
with the problems of getting their independence as rapidly as
possible"—meaning, of course, Egypt, to whom Britain had
given complete independence long before. Nothing could
have been better calculated to sabotage any hope of agreement
in the difficult but not altogether unpromising negotiations
then going on among Britain, France, and Egypt.

Surely, it is time for Americans to realize that to give free rein to their anticolonial sentiment is to play directly into the hands of international Communism in the uncommitted countries. I do not for a moment suggest that the British (or the French or Dutch) record is free of mistakes, stupidities, and even some crimes. But it is not my purpose here to defend that record or to dwell on the past glories of the British Empire—though I believe we have infinitely more to be proud of than to be ashamed of in our imperial and colonial history. The American obsession would be understandable if Americans had once been victims of cruel colonial oppression, or if the U.S. record were free of any taint or tinge of colonialism. But neither is the case. And it might help the government and people of the United States to adopt a more understanding attitude toward their allies, thus leading to more unity of policy in the struggle against world-wide Communist imperialism, if they were to refresh their memory of some episodes in American history.

It might shock them to discover that, in fact, the United States itself has a record of colonialism comparable to that of Great Britain, France, Holland, or Portugal ("colonialism" being defined as the occupation by conquest or settlement and the exercise of sovereignty in lands other than one's own country of origin, inhabited by people of another race and often of a different color). This is not the place to attempt even a summary of that record. I suggest to American readers that they restudy their own history—that they read, for instance, James Truslow Adams' *Epic of America* and Walter Lippman's *U.S. Foreign Policy: Shield of the Republic* for illumination on the American record of colonialism.

Let Americans reflect upon the dealings of U.S. administrations in the nineteenth century with the dark-skinned aborigines of North America, the acquisition of Florida from Spain, the Louisiana Purchase, Polk's settlement of the Oregon dispute, the Mexican War, and the annexation of vast territories from Texas to California. Let them ask them-

selves why, when British troops in the last century crossed
a wide stretch of salt water like the Mediterranean and
occupied someone else's territory in Asia or Africa, that was
a highly reprehensible brand of colonial imperialism; but
when American troops crossed a narrow stretch of fresh
water like the Nueces River and did exactly the same thing
in North America, that was "manifest destiny" and the ful-
fillment of the "American dream." Let them recall how the
United States acquired Alaska, Midway, Pago Pago, and
Hawaii; and let them reread the history of the Spanish-
American War, the *Maine* incident, and the annexation of
Guam, Puerto Rico, and the Philippines. Finally, it might
enlighten them to learn more about the Panama story and
compare U.S. action over that canal with the British and
French actions regarding the Suez Canal that aroused such
righteous indignation in Washington in 1956.

Professor Dunning, a former President of the American
Historical Association, wrote in 1914 of that episode: "The
distinct assumption by the U.S. of the imperialistic character
and responsibilities coincided precisely with the warmest
manifestations of cordiality on the part of Great Britain.
President Roosevelt's Administration (1901–9) teemed with
incidents announcing the new role of the American Republic. The Philippines were relentlessly reduced to order and
subjection; Panama was taken for the sake of the world's
commerce, if incidentally for the specific military and commercial advantage of the taker."

There were not many "warmest manifestations of cordiality" on the part of the United States when, more recently, Great Britain felt prompted to take rather similarly
high-handed action in connection with the Suez Canal. But
Theodore Roosevelt was fortunate in that he did not have
the U.N. General Assembly to deal with in 1902. When he
was criticized for his summary action in another assembly—
the Congress of the United States—he said (according to the

Dictionary of American Biography), "I took the Canal Zone, and let Congress debate and while the debate goes on, the Canal does also." In 1956, there was no dearth of people in England who would have liked to have seen the British Government take the same line with the General Assembly.

It is fortunate for the security of the free world that, both in World War II and still today, the Panama Canal Zone is occupied and guarded by the forces of the United States. But when it comes to moral attitudes about colonialism and talk of the United States being the "moral equal" of the emergent nations of Asia and Africa—and hence, by implication, the moral superior of the British and French— then Englishmen and Frenchmen may perhaps be forgiven for feeling that Americans had better refresh their memories on the story of Panama.

The framework of our shield is unity, without which our common defenses will crumble. If we are to meet and overcome the Communist offensive in the years ahead, it is absolutely vital that we stand together on the problems of Asia, Africa, and Latin America. To do this, we must understand each other, as well as ourselves. Let me take one specific example.

Americans today are very much aware that various white members of the British Commonwealth are now grappling with the terribly complex and difficult problems of the multiracial communities of Africa south and east of the Sahara. I do not for a moment defend the apartheid policy of the present government in South Africa (almost all of whose leaders, by the way, are of Dutch descent); the problem is appallingly difficult, but most of us in Britain think it is being handled in a way that, sooner or later, can only end in disaster. Nor do I suggest that all British settlers in Southern Rhodesia (many of whom are second- and third-generation Rhodesians who, like so many French *colons* in

Algeria, have no other home) have always shown exemplary wisdom; the policy of partnership, accepted in principle in Salisbury, has until recently been honored more in the breach than in the observance. It should be remembered, incidentally, that the Federation of the Rhodesias and Nyasaland—while not yet an independent member of the Commonwealth—enjoys a very large measure of autonomy; and Americans may perhaps recall that many years ago other British settlers, in a remote land inhabited by primitive natives, reacted violently against what they regarded as improper interference in their affairs by the Parliament at Westminster.

On such problems as these, if the American obsession results in a conflict of policy between London and Washington, in widely divergent British and American opinion as expressed in the press and on television and radio, in the adoption by one of the major partners in the Alliance of an attitude of moral superiority to the others—then the only gainer will be the Kremlin, and we will find ourselves in serious danger of losing the Cold War. We *must* stand together, not sacrificing any vital principles, not necessarily taking identical action in every specific instance (which is neither practicable nor, on the whole, desirable), but being guided by a broad common policy, a common approach to the problems—above all, perhaps, by a common emotional and intellectual attitude toward them. I know that this is difficult. But it is no good for Americans to say that their background of freedom from colonial rule is a fact of nature and that they cannot change their way of thinking. Why not? Others have had to. To me and my generation of Englishmen, not so very long ago the imperial tradition seemed a fact of nature: the old British Empire, the "white man's burden," dominion over palm and pine, the Union Jack flying wherever the ship touched land between Southampton and Sidney. We have had to recognize that conditions have changed, and adapt our attitudes to the realities of modern life. Why should Americans be incapable of doing the same?

Americans have their racial problems, too, and not all of us in England think they always handle them wisely. I have already suggested that color discrimination is Communism's best ally. But the British should be very chary of publicly criticizing American actions in conditions entirely alien to our own experience. In return, we in Britain—and even more, our British cousins in Africa—are entitled to ask our American friends to remember that people who live in glass houses should not throw "little rocks."

Chapter *11*

Western Strategy in the Middle East, Far East, and Africa

IT IS NOT EASY for the British, with our long background of association with the Middle East, to adjust to the changed strategic conditions in the area between the Nile and the Persian Gulf. This natural difficulty, plus a failure to realize that total war as an instrument of policy is not part of the Russian plan, has led us into some recent mistakes there. For many years, the Middle East was one of the pillars upon which British global strategy rested. Today, George Kennan is surely right in saying, "Short of the entry of Russian troops into this area, there is nothing that could happen there that would be worth the cost of a world war. With anything else, we could certainly cope."*

I would be reluctant to admit that we could not even cope with that; we have a bad habit of crediting our enemies with

---

* Fifth Reith Lecture, 1957.

the ability to do things that we regard as virtually impossible for ourselves. But I cannot see why Russian troops should want to enter the area. Our own history there since 1918 is not of the sort likely to encourage others to involve themselves in its complexities. (There must have been many occasions when British soldiers and statesmen caught themselves regretting that we had ever taken over the area from the Turks in World War I.) But, in the interval between the wars, it was not only our ingrained imperial habit, not only our practical interest in the freedom of the Canal and the continued flow of oil for the Royal Navy and to the world's markets, but also its new position as the hub of our strategic air routes across the world that endowed the Middle East with such cardinal importance in British policy. All these interests have now assumed a totally different aspect.

Moreover, the Russians have no such interests in the Middle East. They do not need its oil; and the crises of Abadan and Suez have surely proved that the denial of either the oil or access to the Canal can be no more than an expensive inconvenience and serious nuisance to the West. Let us also remember that it is a virtually mortal interest of many Middle East states themselves for the great commercial nations of the West to continue to have the use of the oil and the Canal.

Again, Mr. Kennan: "If we are going to go on bestowing the quality of absolute sovereignty on new political entities at the rate of approximately one a year, as we have been doing for the past fifty years, without much regard for the degree of political maturity and experience which they bring to the exercise of that responsibility, then I think we must expect that armed conflict on a local scale is going to continue to be a frequent feature of the political scene in any area of the world where these raw sovereignties predominate.

The Middle East is such an area."* We must protect our weaker friends and not allow either their property or ours to be stolen. But we no longer have any reason to regard ourselves as the policemen of the Middle East. I do not suggest that we watch with equanimity while the whole area is engulfed by the Communist orbit. There are, however, political and economic means of preventing this—and much better ones than embroiling ourselves in tedious and expensive wars in the area.

But there is one factor that might necessitate our intervention there: Arab-Israeli enmity. The clearer we make this to the Middle Eastern states, the less likely it becomes that we will have to intervene. One of the major tragedies of the past decade was the breakdown of the tripartite agreement of May, 1950, designed to prevent mutual aggression by Israelis or Arabs—a failure that I consider attributable mainly (though not entirely) to weakness and vacillation in Washington. I feel sure that the Israelis—by their intelligence, national unity, and fighting quality—will remain more than a match for their Arab neighbors. But in the event of a formidable combined attempt to destroy Israel, the major nations of the West—and, one would hope, the United Nations also—would be compelled to intervene to preserve the integrity of the small new nation that they themselves brought into existence. It is of equal importance that the peace of the Middle East not be shattered by any move on the part of Israel to extend her frontiers at the expense of her Arab neighbors. If all this is not already clear to those concerned—if, in particular, the Arabs have not yet realized that the state of Israel is there to stay—then the sooner it is made unmistakably plain, the better for the peace of the Middle East. It has suited Russia's policy of fishing in troubled waters to keep alive and exacerbate hostility be-

---

* *Ibid.*

tween the two parties in that part of the world. The Arabs should realize that, if matters were aggravated to the point where a major war arising out of the situation seemed really imminent, the Kremlin would not hesitate to betray them to avoid getting themselves involved.

Meanwhile, I believe Mr. Kennan's advice about the Middle East to be wholly sound. "Let us, of course, do everything we can to discourage hostilities in that part of the world," he tells us. "To this end, let us seek to reconcile and unify where we can, not to divide. But let us at the same time be careful not to place ourselves in a position where such hostilities as cannot be avoided would inevitably have to involve us all."* It is certainly in our interests to foster the economic prosperity of the Middle East by encouraging the development of a wide unified area of trade, agricultural advancement, and industrial cooperation among the various states, whose general well-being and standards of living could so easily be advanced if individual greeds and mutual hatreds and suspicions could only be subordinated to the common good under a more equitable distribution and more civilized exploitation of the vast natural resources of the area. So much could be accomplished by some form of a Middle East Colombo Plan, some Levantine OECD, in which the local states, including Israel, would be the prime movers—while enjoying the full cooperation of the major powers (not necessarily excluding Russia)—in relation not only to local development, but also (and more especially) to the world-wide distribution and marketing of Middle Eastern products. But before anything of this kind can be brought about, the solution must be found—principally by the Middle Eastern states themselves, but also through every form of political and economic pressure from without—to the problem of the displaced Arab refugees. This festering sore has been kept open largely by the Arabs themselves for

* *Ibid.*

political purposes, but they have been aided and abetted by the Soviets, who have made no contribution whatever to alleviate the distress involved, but have merely aggravated it for their own purposes.

In the world outside Europe, perhaps the most critically important need—and, unhappily, one of the most difficult conditions to fulfill—is to arrive at agreement among ourselves in the West on a common approach to the massive problem of China. This becomes more urgent every day—not only on its own merits, not merely because no serious measure of disarmament is practicable without Chinese participation, but also because our failure to agree contains the seeds of really serious divisions in the West and the danger for the United States of "isolation and humiliating diplomatic defeat"[*] in the United Nations.

Here, again, the initiative is as important in politics as in strategy; and it is little less than a disaster that the United States should so largely have surrendered its initiative in this crucially important field to the Kuomintang clique on Formosa. This is a particularly unfortunate example of the implications of one feature of Mr. Dulles' diplomacy—that of basing international policy on moral attitudes. True, we ignore the moral or ethical element at our peril. But the essence of diplomacy surely is that, while it must be directed along the lines of a clear and consistent political strategy, it must retain flexibility and freedom of action in the tactical area. If we take the position that a particular course of action is wicked or immoral (which it might appear to be at the moment), we inevitably find it difficult, if and when expediency requires it, to adapt our tactics to changed circumstances.

It is by now generally accepted—except, perhaps, among

---

[*] James P. Warburg, in a letter to *The New York Times,* January 18, 1961.

a very few extremists and opportunists in Taipeh, that the Chinese revolution is a reality, however brutal and distasteful some of its manifestations may be; that Communist China is potentially, if not actually, the most powerful nation in Asia; and that it is in no sense a satellite of Russia. Among the emergent, uncommitted nations of Asia, there is a widespread feeling of having something in common with the new China, a feeling also of awe and respect (especially since the Korean War) and, to some degree, fear. Some of these nations have large numbers of unassimilated Chinese among their populations who still look on China as their homeland; but none of them wishes to be dominated by China any more than by the West.

It has recently been becoming more clear that, while for the time being China and Russia are linked by the Marxist ideology and it suits them both very well to present a united front against the West, there is little natural affinity between them. It is understandable that Russia should look with growing anxiety upon the prospect of having as neighbors by the end of this century a population of about a billion Chinese, whose eyes could well turn to the great open spaces of the north as well as to the more populated countries of Southeast Asia. And while they do not fear invasion of their East Asian dominions in the near future, there is evidence that the men in the Kremlin are nervous about becoming embroiled in a major war with the West through some impetuous action by Peking.

In a memorandum to a nonofficial international conference* in May, 1956, I wrote: "A sensible and realistic policy toward China would face these facts, and, while we should continue to make it clear that military aggression by China would be met by force, we should accept the fact that China, whether we like it or not, is one of the great powers; that it is useless to base a policy toward her on dislike of Communism, on anger about her action in Korea or resent-

---

* Attended by, among others, Dean Rusk.

ment at her ingratitude for American benevolence in the past; and that the continued nonrecognition of the Peking regime and the 'representation' of China in the United Nations by Chiang Kai-shek's nominee amount to a dangerous farce."

After all, what is—or should be—the medium-range object of our policy in Asia? Is it not that, while being ready to prevent by force the military domination of any part of the world by any one power or combination of powers, we should help the Asian nations themselves to build up a balance of political and economic power in Asia? This depends very largely on creating confidence among them in the West's political common sense, good faith, and disinterested intentions. And a serious obstacle to the winning of that confidence is our present policy vis-à-vis Peking—though India has had some second thoughts since the Tibet affair. In spite of Tibet and minor incursions across the Indian border, however, what we have to fear is not military aggression so much as the emergence within the next ten or twenty years of a China so politically and economically powerful in relation to the present neutral nations that, whether the latter liked it or not, they would have no choice but to go over to the Chinese side of the fence and fall under the domination of Peking.

We cannot prevent this by ostracizing China and giving her no alternative to close cooperation with Russia and the rest of the Communist bloc. It is not in anyone's long-term interest for the anarchy and poverty that has prevailed for so long in China to continue. But our main concern should be to build up a balance in Asia, by fostering the economic strength and fortifying the position of the governments in those emergent nations not yet committed to the Communist way.

To cure an ailment arising from our unrealistic policy of recent years will mean swallowing a bitter pill or two. The first is recognition of Peking and the substitution of a Communist for a Kuomintang man on the Security Council. We really cannot go on much longer with the so-called "moratorium," deferring consideration of the subject by the General Assembly; and the United States would surely be wise to anticipate humiliating defeat by facing the inevitable. Despite some stubborn words, there are indications of a more realistic attitude in the new U.S. Administration (Adlai Stevenson's warning to the Senate Foreign Relations Committee, for instance), while, for the first time, a senior British representative has openly told an American audience that the problem of Chinese Communist representation in the U.N. will have to be solved in the immediate future.

This, of course, cannot involve either handing over Formosa to Peking or the immediate establishment of an independent republic of Taiwan ruled by native Formosans (the two-China policy in a modified form). Surely, the proper solution is the one frequently suggested: a U.N. trusteeship for Formosa for a period during which preparations could be made for a free plebiscite, to enable the people of Formosa themselves to opt either for re-union with China or independent nationhood.

As an immediate step, we should move in the direction of disengagement in this area by putting an end to our dangerous policy on the offshore islands and demilitarizing Quemoy and Matsu, even if it involves evacuation of their populations. Until we get over this admittedly difficult hurdle, we cannot be certain that another crisis in the Far East will not lead to local war, or that limited hostilities in the Straits would not spread by escalation into a world war. Russia, in her own interest, would very likely be on the side of moderation for once. But there is ample evidence that the men in Peking do not dread nuclear war to the same extent as their friends in Moscow; and, indeed, there is some basis for the view that, until China becomes more industrialized and urbanized and hence more vulnerable to nuclear attack, the consequences for that vast country might be less catastrophic than for the more highly developed nations.

This is all very well, I can hear some American friends saying, but what is sauce in the Far East for the American goose is sauce for the British gander: What about Hong Kong?

In the memorandum quoted above, I submitted the following formula as part of a package deal for a future settlement with China: "Without prejudice to the ultimate status and ownership of Hong Kong and subject to the necessary safeguards for the present population and for British commercial and trading rights . . . Hong Kong should become subject to U.N. trusteeship, to be administered by a British governor responsible to the trusteeship council." I have since suggested that it would be a useful contribution to Commonwealth unity—through the assignment of a common responsibility to the member nations—if the internal security of this free international zone were to become the function of a mixed Commonwealth force, on behalf of the United Nations.

I suppose this could be described as another form of disengagement. There are all sorts of arguments against it, some of them powerful, but none, I believe, conclusive. Here is another area where we must face the facts squarely. There are two facts that I dislike about the present situation in Hong Kong. One is that, in the last resort, our policy there depends on our having to defend the indefensible; the other is that if we were ever faced with the issue by China, the only alternatives would be either a humiliating political surrender or a war in which our military object would be impossible to achieve and in which the prospects for support from our allies would be, at best, extremely doubtful. This cannot be considered a sound basis for any policy. In 1997, the leased territories, which form the greater part of the present colony, will revert to China—and then our entire position in Hong Kong will have to be reconsidered anyway. Meanwhile, it is hardly enough to gamble on the probability that our presence in Hong Kong will continue indefinitely to suit the Chinese as well as it does today (the sole guarantee of our present position there). And I find it difficult to believe that the prosperity and security of Hong Kong as a free international zone under U.N. trusteeship would necessarily be less than it is as a British colony.

What of Southeast Asia? I have never been too impressed by the military importance of SEATO; much of the stuffing was taken out of it before its formation by the refusal of the other Colombo powers, notably India, to participate. Nevertheless, it has been a useful symbol of our determination in the Far East and we must continue to make the best of it, despite its inherent limitations. However, there are some provisions in the Manila Treaty that I have always regarded as undesirable and that I think should be modified —specifically, those articles dealing with the so-called "designated states."

In an earlier book, I commented as follows:

Might it not suit us very well if we could have a belt of weak and really neutral States between SEATO and China? I know there is not much chance of real neutrality in the face of Communist subversion and infiltration. But I think there is some reason to believe that it might suit China equally well to have a demilitarized *cordon sanitaire* between her and SEATO. I am inclined to think this is the line on which our policy should be directed. We should firmly establish SEATO as a going concern and leave no one in any doubt that we should fight if Siam were attacked. . . . Meanwhile, as opportunity offers, perhaps with the assistance of

India, we should work toward an agreement with China for the establishment of a neutral zone between us.*

Burma is a determined neutral; and anyone who believes that Laos, Cambodia, and Vietnam would not go to almost any lengths to avoid becoming a battlefield between China and the West—or that the provisions of the Manila Treaty as affecting them have any practical meaning—is deluding himself. Why not face realities and declare them a neutral zone, guaranteed, if possible, by both sides? Something along these lines is currently, if belatedly, under discussion, and one must hope that this is not going to be still another area in which our failure to adopt in time a farseeing and realistic political initiative will result in a setback for us. Some kind of guaranteed neutral zone has recently been proposed by Prince Norodom Sihanouk of Cambodia, and there are indications that it may find favor in Washington. But time marches on, and not to our advantage in this sensitive part of the world.†

Meanwhile, in the Far East, as elsewhere, we must be ready to act forcibly, if the United Nations will not or cannot, against Communist-inspired aggression—as, for instance, by Indonesia against Dutch New Guinea. But if we are to have any hope of support from world opinion there, we should surely now call a halt to Chiang Kai-shek's irresponsible activities within the frontiers of Burma, where he is using American aircraft to support his Kuomintang marauders.

I do not take the view that an attempt to arrive at a reasonable *modus vivendi* with Peking would be taken as a sign of weakness, either in China or in the uncommitted

---

* *The Great Deterrent*, p. 243.

† The guaranteed neutrality of Laos is now the accepted policy of the British and American governments and is the subject of the present negotiations in Geneva. We should surely be considering the extension of this principle to other areas of Southeast Asia, including Vietnam and Korea.

countries of Asia. If it were done in the right way, it is more likely that it would be taken as a sign of common sense and moral courage. Nor do I believe it would have the effect of enhancing the prestige of Peking, to our consequent disadvantage, among the Chinese populations of adjoining countries.

It obviously cannot be taken for granted that Peking would accept the conditions suggested. But we might be able to make it difficult for them to continue to refuse. And at any rate, to do so would put the onus on them and weaken their position in the rest of Asia. On the other hand, for the West to take such an initiative might well transform its whole position in the eyes of the emergent nations.

The African scene is changing so rapidly and the situation in so many parts of that enormous continent at the time of writing is so obscure that it would be rash to attempt any estimate of how it may develop. It is a situation calling for the utmost restraint and discretion on the part of all of us who have no responsibility for dealing with it. The problems are so complex and varied and the tensions so near the surface that statesmen—whether in London or Paris, in Salisbury or Leopoldville—are surely entitled to ask that people with no responsibility at least refrain from making the task more difficult. And outsiders should remember that the only people who can possibly profit from uninformed criticism and interference are the Communists.

There was a recent unfortunate example of this kind of interference. The newly appointed U.S. Assistant Secretary of State for African Affairs, Mennen Williams, on his first official visit to Africa, stepped out of his airplane in Kenya and immediately declared President Kennedy's interest in "Africa for the Africans." He said that they should have self-determination free from the pressures of the Cold War, "at the speed they wanted." (His subsequent insistence that he had meant white and brown, as well as black, Africans was belied by his behavior in Nairobi.) "As far as we are concerned," he added, "that is true of the Rhodesian Federation and the Union of South Africa." All this came at the most crucial moment of a very delicate and highly charged crisis in the relations of the British Government with the governments of both these countries on that very subject. What, one wonders, would Americans have said if Mr. Iain McLeod had arrived in Arkansas at the height of the Little Rock disorders and announced to the press that American Negroes should be admitted to white schools "at the speed they wanted." This sort of thing, so reminiscent of Mr. Stettinius' ill-timed intervention during the 1944 Communist rebellion in Greece,* can only serve to muddy the waters and infuriate America's best friends in Great Britain.

The vital need in the Commonwealth countries of Africa is for courageous statesmanship combining foresight with resolution, strong enough to resist those who would have us go either too fast or too slow. Until recently, we have gone too slow. The principle of multiracial partnership has been scantily honored, and the opportunity may have passed. The countries of Africa east and south of the Sahara cannot do without the white settler, and he is entitled to security in the land he has made his home for several generations (where, indeed, his family may have lived longer than many black settlers). Black Africans cannot prosper without white Africans—in the factories, in the offices, in the mines, and on the farms; nor can they expect real progress for many years without the white administrator. Only one thing is certain: that white domination, which has done so much to build up these countries from primitive barbarism within the memory of living men, must give way to something else—but to what, it is too early to be sure. No one knows better than British statesmen that the old colonialism is completely dead. But those

---

* See Slessor, *The Central Blue*, p. 626.

parts of Africa where the colonial system has not yet given way to some form of self-government remain vulnerable to Communism—like little salients open to attack from three sides. It is in the long-range interest of all, regardless of color, in the struggle for peaceful coexistence, that these salients be evened out as soon as (but not before) an alternative system of government can be established on durable nonracial foundations. The Communists are striving relentlessly to capture them; the least we can hope is that in that effort they will not find allies on our side of the Iron Curtain.

There is no reason why the Commonwealth countries of Africa should go the way of the Congo, provided we learn the right lessons from that calamity. One must hope that the Portuguese will not be too slow to learn those lessons in their territories. If anything were needed to emphasize the supreme importance of a strong United Nations as a force for order and peaceful development in Africa, Khrushchev's attacks on that world body in early 1961 surely served the purpose. Of course, he abused Mr. Hammarskjöld as a "murderer"; of course, he was doing his utmost to reduce to impotence the entire U.N. organization; of course, he wanted to get the U.N. force out of the Congo, leaving it free for exploitation by the Soviets. Communism has a vested interest in misery and chaos, in poverty and anarchy in countries like this; and the United Nations is the best, perhaps the only, hope of curbing and curing them. What could be more natural than for Khrushchev to pour his invective upon the Secretary General and all who support him? So far, it seems likely that he has misplayed his hand and aroused more opposition than support among the uncommitted nations.

My message in this book has been one of toughness combined with flexibility, of hope based on realism. It is not one of enmity to the Russian people—but it is one of utter distrust of their rulers in the Kremlin.

Nevertheless, I have not suggested that we should refuse to negotiate with these men. On the contrary, I have urged that we should meet them, provided we have a practical, constructive policy on which to negotiate—something that, at present, I think we lack. My primary aim has been to suggest such a policy. And my theme is that when we sit down to negotiate with the men of Moscow, we do so from strength, as long as we understand clearly that they will stab us in the back without the slightest compunction if we allow them to imagine they can do so with impunity; that when we sup with the devil, we must use a long spoon—and have a pistol ready at hand.

Postscript on Berlin

KHRUSHCHEV'S MEMORANDUM on Germany, presented to President Kennedy in Vienna, contains a good deal that on the face of it appears not unreasonable. The trouble is, we know from bitter experience that what the Soviets *say* bears little or no relation to what they *do*. They regard international negotiation as a means of achieving their own ends at the expense of other people. And the only thing of which one can be reasonably sure is that their performance will not match their promises. As Kennedy rightly says, "The Soviets and ourselves give different meanings to the same words."

What surely is unfortunate is that once again we have left it to the Russians to take the initiative. It simply is not good enough to reply merely that we are in Berlin by absolute right (though, of course, we are). We must have a constructive policy of our own—and not just stand pat on constitutional rights that mean absolutely nothing to the Kremlin. We used to talk about negotiating from strength. Well, we have the strength. What we don't seem to realize is that another essential in negotiation is a policy. If we have a policy for Germany, it is not apparent to the ordinary man in this country. Immobilism is not a policy. The situation in Germany is not going to stand still. And we, the Western Allies, should take the initiative in the direction of peaceful change—not always leaving it to Moscow to force the pace, or permitting Bonn to obstruct any reasonable move forward.

At any rate, here is what one ordinary man in England would like to see the NATO governments say and do about the Berlin situation.

To the Russians, we should say this: We are perfectly prepared to negotiate with you about Germany or anything else, if and when you are prepared really to negotiate on reasonable terms, instead of merely presenting a list of demands. Your performance at the nuclear test-ban talks and so far in the Laos discussions does not encourage us to believe you are willing to do anything of the sort; but we are ready to try again.

The division of Germany is entirely your fault; you started arming East Germans before we started arming West Germans. Nevertheless, we recognize that partition is now one of the unhappy facts of life. But West Germany is our ally in NATO, and we are not prepared to let the Federal Republic down any more than, apparently, you are prepared to let down the so-called German Democratic Republic, which is your ally in the Warsaw Pact.

Like you, we should be happy to see the two parts of Germany agree between themselves on reunification. But there is not the slightest chance of that as long as you keep twenty divisions in the Eastern zone, a barbed-wire fence between the two parts of Germany, and your grip on the necks of Ulbricht and Grotewohl. As long as that situation pertains, any talk about a free city and symbolic contingents of Allied or neutral troops in Berlin is meaningless. You can show that you mean business by cooperating in the establishment of a zone of arms control under mutual inspection throughout Germany, starting with General Norstad's idea of overlapping screens of inspection posts against surprise attack—Allied on the Eastern and Russian on the Western borders; and leading ultimately to the progressive withdrawal of Russian troops from East Germany and of British, American, and French troops from West Germany—which, incidentally, you your-selves have frequently suggested.

When you have proved by deeds that you can honestly cooperate in some such scheme, then we can discuss whether ultimately West and East Germany can safely withdraw from NATO and the Warsaw Pact respectively, as a preliminary to German reunification. If and when that time comes, we shall propose to you a form of European mutual-security guarantee, to include the provision that any attack on Ger-many, or one by Germany on any of her neighbors, would meet with the combined opposition of all other powers signa-tory to the agreement.

But we are not prepared to see West Germany disappear behind the Iron Curtain.

As for Berlin, if and when there are no longer any foreign armies on German soil, that problem should solve itself; and Berlin could become the capital of a reunified Germany. Meanwhile, our interests in Berlin are that West Berlin must remain free from Communist domination and its people at liberty to support themselves by trading with whom they will. Those are our sole interests, and we regard them as vital.

We are prepared at any time to work out with you—and, if necessary, with neutral representatives—any system (which we think should be applicable to East as well as to West Berlin) that will satisfy us that those interests are adequately safeguarded. Until such a system can be put into effect, our troops will remain there to safeguard them. We have no intention of initiating military operations over Berlin. But if our vital interests in the city are interfered with by force, we shall reply with force. In that event, we shall be fighting not merely for the freedom of the citizens of Berlin, but for the same reason that led Great Britain to declare war on Germany —because we should regard Communist domination of Berlin, like the German attack on Poland, as a sure indication of intent to dominate all Europe. That we should regard as a mortal threat, and react accordingly.

To the West Germans, their partners should say: You are our allies, and we intend to treat you as such. We shall continue to regard an attack on you as an attack on ourselves, even if, in changed circumstances in the future, it is agreed that it would be in the common interest for the two parts of Germany to withdraw from their respective military alignments. We regard the forcible imposition by the Kremlin of a Communist regime in the former Soviet zone as inexcusable; and the reunification of Germany will remain an object of our policy. We do not regard that as unattainable; but neither do we intend to become involved in war to attain it. Our belief in flexibility involves no infirmity of purpose; but we regard a policy that ignores practical reality as worse than useless. Temporary *de facto* recognition of Pankow would merely be acceptance of facts as they are; and we should certainly not regard the substitution of East German for Russian controls on the access to Berlin as itself a *casus belli*. In our view, German reunification can come only by gradual evolution of arrangements between Bonn and Pankow, in circumstances in which direct Soviet control is removed from East Germany; and we regard this continued talk about reunification by free elections as the language of Cloud-Cuckoo-Land.

Finally, we regard it as equally unrealistic to go on talking about Germany's Eastern frontier being decided at some hypothetical peace conference in the unspecified future. We fully accept the assurances of the Government of the Federal Republic that it does not intend to seek the restoration of the "lost territories" by force. But, in our view, to keep that question alive at all is a source of serious instability in Europe, of justifiable suspicion on the part of Germany's neighbors, and potentially of dangerous disunity within the Alliance. We believe the subject to be of interest only to an insignificant minority in Germany itself, and know it to be a matter of indifference to the people of Germany's allies. Western public opinion, when it concerns itself with the matter at all, regards the acquisition by the Poles of the territories beyond the Oder-Neisse line as only reasonable compensation for the terrible wrongs they suffered at the hands of Hitler's Germany. We agree with General de Gaulle that the Federal Republic should accept the Oder-Neisse line as the permanent Eastern frontier of a reunified Germany; and the restoration of the "lost territories" forms no part of our policy.

Meanwhile, we hope the Federal Republic will agree to take a leading part in the establishment of a system of arms control and eventual reduction of forces in the area of Germany as a whole. In our view, it is in that way, and that way only, that a solution can ultimately be found to the problems of reunification of Germany and the permanent freedom of Berlin.

The foregoing will no doubt be open to criticism on the ground of oversimplification of an admittedly complex and difficult subject; and no one imagines that agreement along these lines among the Allies will be easy to achieve.

But is it not about time that we reduced these problems to more simple terms and took a constructive initiative toward solving them, instead of shrouding them in generalizations that are no substitute for policy? In particular, should not we British resume the initiative in formulating Allied strategic policy—an initiative that in recent years we have so largely surrendered?